AF579967

THE TEEN GUIDE TO DATING

One of the greatest areas of concern for a teenager is knowing how to handle a relationship with a member of the opposite sex.

Where do you meet people?
How do you act and what do you say once you have met someone?
Should you go out on blind dates?
How do you handle rejection?
How do *you* break it off with someone without hurting the person's feelings?
Can you just be "friends" with a person of the opposite sex?
Are teen marriages romantic, storybook affairs—or are they something else?
Should you go steady?
What do you do about sex?

These are just a few of the subjects talked about in this straight-from-the hip guide to dating. Throughout the book are examples of real situations that will help you in dealing with your own particular experiences.

OTHER BOOKS BY ELAINE LANDAU

DEATH: Everyone's Heritage
HIDDEN HEROINES: Women in American History
OCCULT VISIONS: A Mystical Gaze into the Future
WOMAN, WOMAN! Feminism in America
YOGA FOR YOU

The Teen Guide to

by Elaine Landau

Published by Julian Messner, a Simon & Schuster Division of Gulf & Western Corporation, Simon & Schuster Building, 1230 Avenue of the Americas, New York, New York 10020

JULIAN MESSNER and colophon are trademarks of Simon & Schuster, registered in the U.S. Patent and Trademark Office.

Manufactured in the United States of America.
Design by Irving Perkins

Library of Congress Cataloging in Publication Data

Landau, Elaine.
The teen guide to dating.

Bibliography: p.
Includes index.
SUMMARY: Contains advice on meeting new people, terrific dates on a tiny budget, handling rejection, friendships between boys and girls, teen marriage, going steady, and sexual involvement.
1. Dating (Social customs)—Juvenile literature. [1. Dating (Social customs)] I. Title.
HQ801.L29 306.7 80-17765
ISBN 0-671-33085-3

For my husband, Bill

Contents

CHAPTER I

How to Meet New People

Someone wants to go out with you. That person may be short or tall, fair or dark, outgoing or shy—you may know him or her well or you may not have met the person yet. Just as there is wisdom in the saying "for every pot there's a cover," one thing is certain: anyone who is willing to put forth some time and creative thought can find a suitable dating partner.

For some people popularity seems to come all too easily. The captain of the football or the basketball team may appear able to capture the hearts of all the girls in school (even the ones he doesn't know personally) without even trying. The prettiest cheerleader on the squad is likely to find her name scribbled across countless notebooks. Those people are often surrounded by groups of seemingly confident individuals who date each other with apparent ease.

Popular individuals aren't the only ones in need of recreation, companionship, and the joy of a fulfilling relationship. Although such individuals may seem to possess superficially desirable qualities, they don't necessarily make the best dating partners or companions. Before you begin your search for a potential boy- or girlfriend it might be a good idea to ask yourself some important questions. What type of person are you? What are some of the things you like to do most? What qualities are you looking for in your date?

Where you'll go to find people to date is largely determined by where you live. Although a large urban center may offer a greater number of people than a small farming community or village, there are desirable people to be found everywhere.

As you spend a good deal of your time at school with others of your approximate age, it is very likely that such a place might prove to be a good source for dating companions. Outside of the typical places to meet people such as in homerooms or classes, the hallways, locker areas, and school cafeteria also afford opportunities to meet new faces and exchange smiles. Perhaps the most valuable place to find others who share similar interests are the curriculum-oriented clubs centered in various schools.

*

Sheila, a sophomore from Asbury Park, New Jersey, had joined the glee club soon after entering high school. A tall girl with a beautiful voice,

Sheila loved to sing and very much enjoyed the special school and community functions at which the glee club entertained. Although Sheila was friendly with a number of girls in the club, she had never met any boys she liked through it until the Christmas the glee club was invited to sing carols at the local senior center.

Ray, a college freshman, was doing volunteer work at the senior center to complete requirements for his college psychology course. It was his responsibility to arrange for the glee club to appear, to make certain transportation was available for everyone, and to serve refreshments after the program. As the performers arrived, Ray noticed Sheila immediately, and Sheila found herself attracted to him as well. When the singing was done, the two chatted over Christmas cookies and hot apple cider and found they had a number of things in common. Although both leaned toward classical music, they went to a rock concert in New York City on their first date and have been dating casually ever since.

*

Greta, a high school senior enrolled in an English Honors class at her school, worked in a special after-school program tutoring students in reading at the local elementary school. Greta, who taught creatively using materials her students enjoyed reading, soon gained a reputation as an extremely successful tutor. Bill, another student tutor from Greta's school, was fascinated by her teaching approach and was determined to know her better. After several conversations with her, Bill became fascinated by Greta's personality as well and asked her to a party on the following Saturday.

Many town or village agencies offer programs for young people which enable them to meet new people as well as develop new interests and hobbies. Often local libraries offer a wide variety of workshops. Tuckahoe Public Library in Tuckahoe, New York, gives a series of classes in gourmet cooking for teens. Jeannie, a high school senior from a neighboring town, signed up for a number of the cooking workshops. Although no young men attended the sessions, Jeannie did meet Irene, a senior from Tuckahoe High School who shared her fervor for the culinary arts.

The two became fast friends and decided to host a brunch together featuring several of the more exotic dishes they had learned to create. Irene invited her boyfriend, Larry, as well as her brother, Fred, thinking that he and Jeanie might like each other. The foursome enjoyed a pleasant afternoon, but there were hardly fireworks between Fred and Jeannie. However, Jeannie had found a good friend in Irene, whose company she genuinely enjoyed. As Irene and Larry went to a different high school, Jeannie had an opportunity to meet a variety of interesting new people through them as time passed. One of Larry's basketball teammates, Bob, liked Jeannie so much that after several dates he invited her to his senior prom.

*

A New Jersey library recently offered a workshop in T-shirt printing for teens. It was an enjoyable Saturday afternoon as well as an excellent opportunity to get acquainted. Often libraries sponsor teen book discussions or rap groups, which may serve as vehicles to facilitate new friendships.

The settings of certain types of business establishments are especially conducive to meeting members of the opposite sex. Poster-novelty shops, record stores, fast-food chains, and sporting goods establishments are all good bets. Many church and synagogue groups have special youth clubs for teen members of their congregations. Often these youth divisions have county and state affiliations; regional conventions as well as special trips offer the possibility of meeting still more individuals. It is always a good idea to volunteer to do work on the various special committees these groups usually have. Not only does this help to keep you better-informed about newly planned events, but it often puts you at a better vantage point to initiate new friendships.

One spring the teen group at Christine's church decided to put on a carnival for the younger children in town. Having volunteered to serve on the food and entertainment committee, Christine had the responsibility of approaching various group members to see if they would be willing to help with the festivities.

To operate the wheel of fortune, Christine called

Tim, a high school senior whom she had been extremely anxious to meet for the past few months. He agreed to do the job and immediately saw the necessity of meeting with Chris on several occasions to work out the format and scheduling of his new endeavor. Chris soon found that Sandy, an equally attractive junior from a neighboring high school, was just as anxious to meet with her before the carnival to learn more about running the ring toss game.

Some employment situations especially lend themselves to meeting new people. By the time Wendy was a high school senior, she felt ready to date college boys but found it difficult to meet them. At a friend's suggestion she applied for a job in the library of a local junior college. Wendy worked at the library's circulation desk two days after school and all day Saturday. As most of the college students used the library to complete their homework assignments, Wendy met scores of new people. Checking the books in and out gave her the opportunity to initiate conversations with the students by commenting on the various library materials they selected.

Even if you aren't interested in an employment situation, local college libraries are often excellent places to meet new people. Many colleges allow the public to use their libraries free of charge. In addition to housing fine volumes, libraries also often house much of the student body on weekends.

In between conversations across table tops, you'll have an opportunity to work on your own school assignments. You may find that your grades and the number of people you meet rise simultaneously.

Counselor positions at summer camp are often good spots to meet peers of the opposite sex. Many camps employ high school students during the summer to assist the teachers and other staff. Often the camps hire former campers who they feel will do an especially good job. The summer of her junior year of high school, Rita got a job at Camp Padwee, a small Rhode Island camp where she had spent her summers when she was younger. Rita was thrilled to learn that she, along with several other junior counselors, would be assisting the archery instructor, a tall graduate student named Dirk. Rita loved working with the children, and in the process of helping them follow Dirk's instructions, she became quite a skilled archer herself.

During the first few weeks of camp, Rita spent a good deal of time initiating conversations with Dirk, not to mention getting up at 5:30 A.M. to make certain she had ample time to blow dry her hair and apply her makeup before camp started for the day. At best Dirk's reactions could be described as polite. He listened to her thoughts, answered her questions cheerfully, and then went about his business without so much as ever asking Rita if she'd like to go out for coffee. Rita became a bit discouraged, but she didn't give up. She simply reinforced her efforts—more conversation and more eye makeup. She didn't renounce her quest completely until the second Sunday in July—Visitor's Day.

Visitor's Day at Camp Padwee was a festive time when the parents and families of the campers visited the camp and participated in a series of day-long activities. Many of the camp's teachers and instructors would bring their spouses and families to meet the others and join in the fun. When Dirk showed up with a beautiful slender woman named Diana whom he introduced as his fiancée, Rita decided to give up. Even her most expensive mascara wand would not help her now.

Rita consoled herself with the fact that she had enjoyed her experience at camp, become a skilled archer, earned money, and made some wonderful new friends. She decided to spend most of the afternoon of Visitor's Day with one such friend named Lenny, another junior counselor who had worked on the archery field with Rita and Dirk. Lenny had a wonderful sense of humor, and when Rita confided to him how she had felt about Dirk, he cheered her up. She began to feel really great when he asked her to a movie on Saturday night.

Parks, zoos, and nature sanctuaries are often excellent places to meet new people. Some individuals have had really good luck joining hiking clubs or canoeing groups. In the summer many municipalities have special teen recreational programs that offer additional opportunities. In most areas you can have a lot of fun meeting new people at the local swimming pool. Summertime is vacation time, and people you already know often invite guests from surrounding communities to swim with them.

Doing things is crucial in forming new relationships. You'll never meet anyone sitting at home alone in your room. It's imperative to put yourself in situations where there are other people of your age group.

Although it's certainly important to be at the right place at the right time, never underestimate the value of attitude when you're facing the challenge of meeting new people. The attitude you exhibit can tell another more about you than the clothes you have on. Do you have a cheerful smile or do you just laugh nervously? When approached by a member of the opposite sex at a social function, do you have a warm response ready that will help the conversation flow or do you shift your weight nervously from foot to foot anxiously wishing you were anywhere but there and answer with a one or two word reply that puts an abrupt end to further conversation?

Warmth and enthusiasm are essential qualities in forming a relationship. A genuinely approachable person is one who is receptive and kind—someone who can make another feel comfortable and secure in his or her company. It's a person who remembers when someone was concerned about a math test on Wednesday morning and makes sure to inquire how things went that afternoon. This sort of person is considered likable by members of both sexes. He or she is an open person—an individual able to give, share, and really hear what another has to say.

Being in the right situation to meet someone is important, but not as important as what you bring to that situation. In fact, very often people with the right attitude create situations in which they are very likely to meet others.

*

Bob, a college freshman, was enroute to his home in New Jersey from the university he attended in Washington D.C., when the train he was riding suddenly stopped midway to his destination. There had been an accident involving another train earlier that afternoon, and the conductor announced that Bob's train would be indefinitely delayed. It was a very warm day, and before long the passengers' tempers rose with the temperature.

The reactions of the different riders varied. After only twenty minutes, one man rapidly paced up and down the aisle loudly insisting that the train company immediately engage helicopters to transport the passengers from the railcars to their destinations. A young female college student decided to use the time to study. One college senior took out his guitar, and the group of students accompanying him on the trip sang.

Bob, who had recently broken up with his girl friend, decided that this might be a good time to try to meet some new people. After all, the unusual delay had created an atmosphere in which standard proprieties seemed relaxed. Bob felt that people might be more approachable in this type of situation and decided to try his luck.

He got out of his seat to stretch his legs and walked to the no-smoking car. There in an aisle seat towards the front of the car sat a tall girl with green eyes and long red hair that hung down to her waist. Her peach-colored complexion and brilliant smile were enough to send Bob straight to her seat. As he approached the girl, Bob noticed that she wore a necklace with the name Sandra on it.

Flashing his brightest smile, Bob bent over, extended his hand, and said, "Hi, Sandy." At the very sound of his voice, Sandra's face took on an expression of extraordinary displeasure. To Bob's overture she speedily replied, "Get lost, you creep," and with comparable directness turned her body toward the window, away from the aisle and Bob.

Bob handled the situation extremely well. He simply said, "Sorry, I just thought I'd like to meet you," and then returned to his seat. Bob had sufficient good judgment and self-confidence not to take the rejection too seriously. There was nothing wrong with him or the manner in which he had tried to meet Sandra; she simply had been unapproachable that day. Even if Sandra had not wanted to meet Bob, it was she and not Bob who handled the whole situation tactlessly.

After returning to his seat, Bob decided to join the group of young people singing folk songs. They so enjoyed themselves that the group continued their serenade even after the train began to roll again. When everyone was finally exhausted, and the musician put his guitar away, Marsha, one of the female singers, struck up a conversation with Bob. Although they had never met before, the two soon learned that they attended the same university and lived within blocks of each other. They exchanged telephone numbers and promised to get in touch with one another when they returned to school after the vacation. In spite of the train delay and Sandra's attitude, when Bob arrived at his parents' home that evening, he felt as though he had had a wonderful day. He had remained open to new possibilities, and as a result, something new and exciting had happened to him.

CHAPTER 

Matchmaker, Matchmaker . . .

The blind date is a time-honored practice that has survived through the ages. If you haven't been on at least one already, it is very unlikely that you will go through life without someone at some time saying, "Hey, I just met someone who'd be perfect for you."

Various forms of this practice exist among different groups. In some cultures marriages are still prearranged. When a child reaches the age deemed appropriate for matrimony, his or her parents will seek out the services of a matchmaker. For a monetary sum, the matchmaker creates couples by introducing young people who appear to complement one another. After the introduction, the new couple will often embark upon a series of highly supervised dates. If they like each other their relationship will lead to marriage. If not, each will return to the matchmaker for further introductions.

Professional matchmakers still exist in modern America as well. Often these individuals are approached not only by young people desiring marriage, but by single, widowed, and divorced people of all ages. Many of the matches are more casual than those made by traditional matchmakers in cultures where prearranged marriage is still the prevalent mode. Individuals are brought together according to preferences and tastes. Telephone numbers are usually exchanged, and the couple begins to date.

In many large cities there are scientific dating services which claim to match people by computer. Date-A-Match is a popular New York City dating service. Interested applicants answer a telephone questionnaire and then, for a fee, are sent the telephone numbers of other applicants which the service deems suitable for them.

The blind date is actually just a casual mode of more formalized matchmaking. Many people claim to greatly enjoy blind dates and actively seek them out. There are several distinct advantages to the blind date or "fix up," as it is commonly referred to. For one thing, the blind date removes the pressure and tension usually found in the initial meeting situation. You don't have to walk across a dance floor to introduce yourself and then worry about possible rejection. With a blind date you are guaranteed a date, or at the very least a phone call.

Fix ups also eliminate much of the mystery involved in getting to know a new person. Usually, you are able to find out in advance whether the individual shares some of your interests, likes, and dislikes. For example, a friend you met on the swim team might be likely to fix you up with someone who enjoys swimming and aquatic sports as much as you do. Similiarly, a fellow hiker might know other people who enjoy the outdoors.

Perhaps the best reason for accepting a blind date is because someone you trust has singled out a person he or she feels would be especially right for you. Often it is necessary to date a number of people before you find someone you enjoy spending time with. In arranging a blind date a third party has felt that you and the new person will get along well together. And if the person making the match knows the two people involved well, he or she may be right.

It isn't always necessary to wait for someone else to play matchmaker if you are interested in meeting new people through blind dates. If one of your friends develops a new romantic interest in someone from another circle, it is perfectly acceptable to inquire if that person has any interesting and available friends.

*

Two of Sharon's closest friends, Sonia and Monica, were a year older than she and, as a result, entered college while Sharon was still a senior in high school. Sonia went to an out-of-state school about sixty miles away where she lived in a dormitory, while Monica attended the local college and continued to live at home.

Sonia thoroughly enjoyed the social aspects of her new college experience. She met a number of interesting boys and wrote glowing reports to Sharon about each of them. After Sonia adjusted to her new academic schedule, she decided to invite Sharon up to visit her on several different weekends. Sharon was very excited about getting a close-up view of the college she herself had been thinking of attending the following year, as well as delighted at the prospect of seeing her good friend again so soon.

On the first weekend Sharon arrived, Sonia introduced her to Ted, a college junior she had been seeing quite frequently. Sharon had hardly finished unpacking her overnight bag when Ted informed her that he had arranged a blind date for her that very evening with one of his fraternity brothers, a man named Ray. Ted assured Sharon that Ray possessed all the qualities she had ever hoped to find in a man. He told the girls that he and Ray would pick them up at eight o'clock.

The idea of the blind date excited Sharon, but she felt a little flustered by all the sudden attention. She wondered how Ted, whom she had only just met, could possibly know "all the qualities she had ever hoped to find in a man."

After discussing her feelings with Sonia, Sharon learned that quite a bit of forethought and preparation had gone into her planned date with Ray. Sonia had told Ted several weeks earlier that she was going to invite Sharon up to the college. She described Sharon to Ted in detail and asked if he could possibly find a suitable date for her. Ted remarked that Sharon sounded like a lovely girl and added that the situation would not pose a problem.

But Sonia was not content to leave the matter

solely to Ted. She asked if she could take part in the selection process or at least hear a bit more about the boy Ted had chosen. Ted and Sonia discussed all their mutual male friends at great length. After eliminating those with steady girlfriends, they decided on Ray for a number of reasons. Ray had a great sense of humor, and Sharon loved to joke and tease. Ray was very athletic, while Sharon had been on her high school girls' soccer and track teams for two years. Both were terrible dancers and shared an avid dislike for discos. And both liked to date tall people—Sharon was five feet nine inches, Ray was six feet three inches.

After hearing about Ray from Sonia, Sharon was quite anxious to meet him. When their date was over, she had not been disappointed. The two seemed to take to one another. They exchanged addresses and corresponded until Sharon's next visit to the college. Sonia did not need to get any further blind dates for Sharon. Every time Sharon visited Sonia she saw Ray. In fact, Sharon and Ray continued to date throughout much of the year, long after Ted and Sonia had broken up.

Sharon had not expected Monica, her other close friend, to be very helpful in arranging new social opportunities for her. Monica was a local girl attending the local junior college, and Sharon reasoned that the boys at Monica's school would be boys from her hometown whom she already knew. However, the situation turned out quite differently. Although quite a number of local students attended the college, many others came from different parts of the state and lived in dormitories. There were numerous parties and social functions given on campus, and Monica proved to be quite popular.

While in Sonia's case it had been she who had initiated finding a blind date for Sharon, one of the boys Monica was dating asked her if she knew a nice girl for his roommate, Jeff. Monica immediately thought of Sharon. When Monica spoke to her about it, Sharon agreed to the introduction. Although she had already been seeing Ray for several months, they were not going steady. Sharon's parents were quite fond of Ray, but they were anxious for her to see other boys as well.

Monica did not know very much about Jeff and made very little effort to find out more. She did learn that he was a biology major and an exceptional student and passed this information on to Sharon. Monica had told her boyfriend to tell Jeff that Sharon loved the outdoors, so when Jeff spoke to Sharon he suggested a Sunday hike and picnic. Sharon thought this was a wonderful idea. Remembering her favorable experience with Ray, she anxiously looked forward to her new blind date on Sunday.

The sight that greeted Sharon when Jeff rang her bell that Sunday morning was that of a short pale boy who stood nervously before her with his hands dug deep into his pockets as he shifted his weight from foot to foot. When he saw Sharon he squeaked out a barely audible hello, and she invited him in. After meeting Sharon's parents, the two drove to the camping and hiking area.

There was little conversation in the car. Sharon thought Jeff was a nervous driver, as he narrowly missed hitting two cars along the way. She didn't know whether Jeff always drove that way or whether he was just nervous because of the date, but in either case she felt it was unwise to pursue the conversation and distract Jeff from his driving.

When they finally arrived, things did not greatly improve. Jeff experienced difficulty walking up the steep hill to the picnic grounds. He had never hiked before and had not worn the proper shoes. Sharon, a veteran hiker, tactfully slowed her pace to wait for him.

Unfortunately, the picnic itself went on quietly and quickly. At this point, Sharon tried to spark the conversation between Jeff and herself, but to little avail. Jeff gave one-word answers to most of Sharon's queries. For example, when she asked if he had any hobbies, he simply replied, "no." After a while Sharon grew tired of hearing herself speak and felt extremely frustrated by the entire experience. She gave up on salvaging the afternoon. She helped Jeff pack up the picnic things, and the two went quietly to the car—only on the way back Sharon took less care to be certain that Jeff was able to keep up with her.

During the ride back Jeff did not say a word to Sharon. She sat smoldering in her seat the whole time. When he walked her to her door, Jeff leaned forward as if to kiss her, but Sharon quickly stepped aside. Jeff suddenly blurted out, "Well, when do you want to go out again?" Sharon was both astonished and insulted. Flashing an icy smile, she replied, "never," stepped into her house, and closed the door behind her. Once in her room Sharon angrily recounted the events of the day. "Well, he certainly has a lot of nerve," she thought. "He doesn't say a word to me all day, acts as if I don't exist, and then expects me to go out with him again."

Sharon resolved to forget the whole unpleasant incident, but that night a telephone call from Monica brought the matter to mind once again. Monica chided Sharon for treating Jeff so harshly. She remarked that Jeff had returned to the campus feeling both shocked and hurt. He told Monica and his roommate that he thought Sharon was one of the most beautiful girls he had ever seen. He felt honored to have had the opportunity to take her out and had wanted very much to see her again. He had added that he didn't understand how a girl with so much sparkle could be so cruel.

Sharon was dumbfounded by Monica's report of Jeff's reaction. She simply said to Monica, "Why, that's incredible, I don't believe it," and went on to report the boring events of the afternoon.

How could two people out together interpret the experience so differently? Could anything have been done to salvage the afternoon? Should Sharon and Jeff have been matched up to begin with?

It is quite possible for two people to spend an afternoon together and evaluate the day differently. Often our perception of an event is based on a combination of our expectations and our past experiences. Jeff's previous dating experiences differed radically from Sharon's. He was a shy, quiet boy, who had only gone out with two other girls in his life. Both girls were also shy, not terribly attractive, and neither was very adept at conversation. Jeff thought lively, sparkling, romantic interchanges were reserved for the movies and passionate paperback books. He believed that a date was successful if two people simply enjoyed an activity together.

Sharon, on the other hand, was an affable, outgoing girl who had been dating since she was twelve years old. She was popular throughout high school, often becoming close friends with older students. Being a bright, articulate, and mature young woman, Sharon frequently dated boys who were several years older than herself. She was also strikingly beautiful.

To Jeff, Sharon was a dream come true. He had never hoped to date anyone as lovely as she and after seeing her he felt extremely grateful for the opportunity to go out with her. It didn't matter that the conversation hadn't flowed between them. Conversation never flowed when Jeff spoke to anyone.

Sharon explained to her friend Monica that she would have never become so angry at Jeff if she had realized initially how terribly shy he was. She even told Monica that at one point she didn't know if Jeff was stuck up or just plain rude because of what she had interpreted as his ignoring her. By the end of their telephone conversation, Monica admitted that she herself hadn't known very much about Jeff's personality to begin with.

Perhaps the disastrous afternoon and the hurt feelings could have been avoided if a bit more investigation had been done prior to the date. It was Monica's responsibility to learn more about Jeff before suggesting him to Sharon, and it was Sharon's responsibility to make certain she knew enough about him before accepting the date. Neither girl acted as maturely as she might have in this situation.

It is often difficult to find out what someone is really like through secondhand sources. However, there are some precautions you can take to insure a higher degree of success when accepting blind dates. Make sure you know the person who is doing the matchmaking. Do you like or admire that individual? Do you trust and respect his or her judgment?

Pam, a high school sophomore, once accepted a blind date from a girl she hardly knew. The boy turned out to be that girl's cousin, a fellow who had earned himself a reputation for being loud, rude, and abusive. When none of her own friends would accept a date with her cousin, the girl called Pam whom she knew only casually from school. Pam, who hadn't gone out in a long time, was anxious to meet someone new and quickly accepted the offer. Even a year later Pam still recalled that date as one of the most memorable events of her life. She claimed she couldn't remember a more dreadful evening.

Although it is always a good idea to remain open minded and not be overly judgmental when meeting new people, it is important to maintain certain standards for the kind of treatment you expect. In evaluating whether or not to accept a blind date, it may be helpful to devise two separate lists. On the first list write down the things you absolutely do not like in a dating partner. Keep this list short—try to limit it to three items. As it is important to concentrate on the positive rather than the negative, make certain your sheet of paper contains only things that you feel very strongly about.

For example, Miriam, a Jewish girl from New York City, had had an extremely religious upbringing. She had always lived in Jewish neighborhoods, attended private Hebrew schools, observed all religious holidays, and enjoyed a close circle of Jewish friends who believed strongly in their faith. During the summers she visited her grandparents in Israel and she hoped one day to teach at Hebrew University in Jerusalem.

Although interfaith dating might be right for others, both Miriam and her parents felt it was out of the question for her. For Miriam, Judaism was much more than a religion; it was a way of life, and she felt it was crucial that anyone whom she dated share her beliefs.

One day when leaving her ballet class, Miriam happened to walk out with another student who was being picked up by her older brother. The brother saw the girls, took one look at Miriam, and flashed a smile that didn't leave his face throughout the long ride home. After questioning his sister about Miriam, he simply said, "Tell her I'm interested." The next week at ballet class that's exactly what the girl did.

Miriam told the girl that she was flattered by her brother's attention and asked her to thank him for his interest. She went on to explain her preference in dating only Orthodox Jewish boys. The girl understood her position and respected Miriam for her honesty.

*

Angela and Joan are two seniors attending the same high school in Colorado. The girls have been friends for a number of years. Sometimes people mistake them for sisters as they look somewhat alike and both are over five feet ten inches tall. Angela considers height when selecting dating partners. It is important to her that the boys she goes out with are at least as tall as she. Angela finds it extremely difficult even to try to date someone shorter. When she has attempted to in the past, she's felt uncomfortable and tended to slouch. Angela does not see this requirement as an insurmountable problem. Although it does limit the number of potential dating partners available to her, she does claim there are sufficient numbers of tall boys available. On her dating list of things that are unacceptable to her, she might, therefore, wish to list short boys.

Although Joan is the same height as Angela, she handles the situation quite differently. It simply does not matter to Joan how short or tall any individual is. According to Joan, "I think a guy is good looking if he looks good to me. It doesn't matter how high he stands as long as the whole package looks good. White teeth and beautiful smiles are what turn me on. I also go for big blue eyes. I once went out with a guy who had the most terrific pair of blue eyes. I loved his long black lashes. He was sensational looking and really knew how to play the guitar to boot. It never mattered to either of us that he was about a head shorter than I was."

*

Some people are very lucky. They can't think of a single thing to put on their list of qualities they wish to avoid in a dating partner. In a way they are very fortunate to be so open to new people and experiences. However, if there are some things you are certain you don't want in a dating partner, don't feel badly about it. You are entitled to have certain preferences and being aware of these will be very helpful to you in selecting partners. Whether a friend solicits you for a blind date or whether you actively ask your friends if they know anyone who might be right for you, it is important to be open about what you expect.

On the other list write down all the things you'd like in a dating partner. Jim, a high school junior from California, made a list that read something like this: long blond hair, slender body build, sweetness, a sense of humor, big brown eyes, athletic ability, and an interest in outdoor water sports. This list is designed to give you and your matchmaking friends an idea of what your dream person would be like. It is important not to cling rigidly to this list. If you are able to find a person who possesses two out of five qualities from your list consider yourself very fortunate. Jim was very lucky in finding Sandra, a blind date he met through one of his surfing friends. Sandra had everything he wanted in a girl—she was attractive, fun loving, and shared many of his interests. Jim has now been dating her for over a year and a half, and every time he looks into her green eyes he can't understand why he ever liked brown-eyed girls.

Make your friends aware of the things you like in a dating partner as well as the fact that you are interested in meeting new people. Even if they don't know of anyone right now, they may meet someone in the future who is just right for you, and you will come to mind.

What you do on a blind date is another important element in helping to insure its success. Remember that on a blind date you have to spend several hours with someone you have never seen in your life. It is possible that the two of you may just hit it off and that conversation will flow easily between you. However, to help facilitate the evening, it is always a good idea to have a specific activity planned. Try to choose an activity that you can talk about afterward, just in case you find you have nothing else in common to discuss. It is a better idea to go to a movie or disco roller skating than to take a long drive in the country.

*

Karen, a high school senior from New York City, visited her cousin one summer at a beach resort near Asbury Park, New Jersey. Her cousin Helen was a popular girl who enjoyed the attention of a number of boys. Helen, an avid swimmer, spent most of her summer days on the beach. Karen joined her for a daily routine of swimming, tanning, and playing volleyball on the sand. In the evenings there were cookouts and beach parties.

Cliff, one of the boys Helen was seeing, was a

lifeguard at a local beach. After meeting Karen at a party, Cliff suggested to Helen that they match Karen up with his brother Bill, another lifeguard at a neighboring beach. Bill picked Karen up at 7:30 P.M. as Helen had told her he would. Karen was immediately impressed with Bill's good looks and outgoing personality. Bill whisked her out the door, and when Karen asked where they were going, Bill suggested a walk along the beach. Karen consented.

During the car ride to the beach Bill described all his exploits as a lifeguard to Karen. Once they arrived at the shore, the setting provided a perfect background for Bill's continued explanation of his heroics. He never once asked Karen anything about herself.

Bill's whole saga took almost twenty minutes. After that the couple walked hand in hand along the beach watching the waves roll in and out. It didn't take Karen long to realize that Bill's only further intention for the evening's activity was just to roll around in the sand with her. In fact—in keeping with his strong lifeguard image—he practically knocked her down on the sand to do so. Karen wanted no part of it. She felt she hardly knew Bill and, handsome as he was, she had no desire to share even the slightest intimacy with someone who was practically a stranger. When she asked him if he wanted to do anything else that evening, Bill replied, "What else is there to do?" Karen suggested that a swift trip home might be a good idea.

After that evening Bill and Karen never saw each other again. It is ironic that the evening went so poorly, since most people who know them would

agree that as individuals both Bill and Karen are lovely people. Why their personalities clashed so badly that evening has a lot to do with how the date was set up.

For one thing, the date was entirely arranged by Karen's cousin. Helen had told Bill what day and at what time to pick up her cousin. If Bill had simply been given Karen's telephone number, he could have spoken to her in advance of the date. It would have been Karen's responsibility to ask where they were going that evening. If Bill told her a walk along the beach, she could have suggested an alternate activity that might have kept them better occupied, such as a game of miniature golf or a trip to one of the local amusement parks. If Bill held to his initial suggestion and made it clear to Karen that he wasn't interested in anything except walking along a dark beach with her, she could have declined the date and saved them both an unpleasant and disappointing evening. As a rule, blind dates tend to be far more successful if the couple speak to one another before the date and a mutually enjoyable activity is agreed upon.

Some people find it difficult to spend an entire evening alone with someone they've never seen before even if they are engaged in an agreeable activity. If you feel that way, it may be possible to take your blind date out on a group date. It's a good idea sometimes to arrange a double date with the couple that made the match. Often they know both of the new people involved and the friendship can help to facilitate conversation. If the couple is unavailable or if you were matched up by an individual who isn't currently dating anyone, it is still possible to arrange a group activity for your date.

*

Phil, a high school senior from Massachusetts who had recently broken up with his girl friend, asked one of his friends on his football team if he knew any new girls. His friend said he would ask his girl friend, but, as it turned out, all her friends were already going with people.

When that lead turned up a zero, Phil's friend asked his sister if she knew of anyone available for Phil. His friend's sister claimed she knew the perfect girl for Phil, a very pretty high school junior named Janet from a nearby school whom she had met in her body movement class. Phil's friend didn't know Janet and his friend's sister wasn't seeing anyone at the time, so a double date was out of the question. As Phil felt the evening would have a better chance of being successful if he and Janet could spend it around others, he invited her to a hayride sponsored by the youth group at his church.

Their evening together proved to be quite delightful. Janet greatly enjoyed the hayride and the cookout that followed. Phil's friends from church made her feel very much at home. In addition to getting to know and like Phil, Janet met several girls she later became friends with. Phil and Janet had much in common and found quite a lot to talk about. Still, the relaxed and comfortable atmosphere of the hayride helped to get things off on the right track.

Even if you are matched up by a close and reliable friend, talk to your date in advance on the phone, and select an absorbing activity for the evening, there is still no absolute guarantee that your blind date will turn out to be a pure delight. Margie, a high school sophomore, took all those precautions and was still bitterly disappointed in her experience.

When Margie first spoke to Bert, a high school junior who had been given her telephone number, she was quite impressed. The conversation was lively, and Bert seemed to have a terrific sense of humor. In fact, Margie was so taken with him that when he asked her what she'd like to do on the evening of their first date, she suggested that they go to the St. Valentine's Day Dance being given at her school. Margie just had the feeling that Bert was the kind of guy she'd like to show off to all her friends. He had mentioned to her on the phone that he was a little hefty, but Margie just adored the masculine build of football players and reasoned that Bert must look like that.

When Margie came down the stairs the Saturday night of their date to greet Bert, she wanted to run right back up to her room. "Hefty" was simply not the word to describe Bert. Margie thought in her frustration, "that guy must weigh at least three hundred pounds." When Margie told him it was a Saturday night dance, she had just assumed that he would dress appropriately. She herself had bought a new pair of white satin disco pants and a red silk top for the occasion. She had had her hair done at the beauty shop that afternoon, and her long black mane hung to her shoulders partially braided and adorned with bright red ribbons. Bert, on the other hand, had arrived wearing torn jeans and a greasy T-shirt. His sense of humor was still apparent; as Margie entered the room he was busily entertaining her parents with funny stories. But at the moment, nothing seemed very humorous to Margie.

It was obvious that Bert was impressed with Margie when she walked into the room. He flashed her a big smile, revealing that several of his teeth were missing. At that moment Margie felt that she wanted to die. She just couldn't stand the idea of bringing him to her school dance and was at a loss at what to do. Excusing herself, she asked her mother if she could speak to her in the kitchen.

She explained her feelings to her mother and asked her if she felt it would be too rude to ask Bert to take her somewhere else. Her mother replied that Bert seemed to be a nice enough boy, and that she felt ashamed of her own daughter for condemning another person on superficialities. She added that Bert was quite entertaining and had been keeping her and Margie's father laughing for about fifteen minutes.

Margie felt infuriated. Hadn't her mother always told her that a person's appearance counted a great deal? Besides, wasn't it her parents who had paid for her beautiful new disco outfit and for her to have her hair done for this date?

Marching out of the house with Bert, Margie was still unsure as to what she should do. But once in his car, she remembered a famous line from a Shakespearen play she had studied in school—"To thine own self be true." Finally deciding that she wanted to be someplace with Bert where she could feel comfortable, Margie blurted out, "Bert, do you think it would be all right if we went to a movie instead of the dance?" Judging from Bert's appearance, Margie felt she would be best off with him in a darkened movie house. Perhaps fortunately for everyone, Bert did not understand Margie's true intention and simply thought she felt like seeing a movie. Anxious to please her, he drove to the nearest theater.

Ironically, Margie had a wonderful time that evening. Bert kept making jokes throughout the movie and Margie found him to be funnier than the comedians on the screen. However, when Bert called her for a second date the following week, she graciously declined his offer. Margie did what was right for her in her predicament. Fortunately, she was able to do so without hurting another person's feelings.

Blind dates always involve the element of the unknown. It's simply part of the risk involved for the opportunity to perhaps meet someone you'd like to date. If a situation arises that you simply cannot tolerate, don't chide yourself for your feelings. You are a unique person with your own set of values. You are entitled to your own opinion and reactions. Simply try to extricate yourself without unnecessarily hurting anyone else.

Don't be shy about accepting or actively recruiting blind dates for yourself. There's certainly as much chance of one being a success as a disaster, and although many blind dates never get past the first evening, some evolve into long and fulfilling relationships. Combine your courage and sense of adventure with a few beforehand precautions, and you'll embark on your blind dates less blindly.

CHAPTER 

Terrific Times on a Tiny Budget

❀ When you're not dating anyone, your world may seem to center around obtaining a date. You may daydream of going steady with someone really terrific, or perhaps your fantasy includes a variety of dating partners all of whom are look alikes for your favorite film stars. At times you may believe that your every problem would vanish if you only had someone to go out with. However, in reality these thoughts are very far from the truth.

Dating, whether it's with one special person or a number of people, has its own set of complications. Often the success of the date, especially when you're seeing a new person, has a great deal to do with the activity selected for the evening. On a date two different people have to be pleased and entertained. They may enjoy some mutual things and may have much in common, but at times it's difficult to find this out before they meet.

There's also the question of money. With unlimited funds available, it isn't difficult to plan a fantastic evening. However, most people have to live within monetary limits, and often these limits can be quite confining. Yet it is still possible to have an enjoyable evening without spending a tremendous amount of money.

Just as geographic location will help to determine the number and type of people you will meet, where you live also greatly influences the type of entertainment available to you. No matter whether you live in the country or the city, though, the idea behind going out on a date is to have a good time with someone you like. If you are able to break away from some of the more conventional concepts of what a typical date should be, you will find quite a bit available to you.

We live in an age of athletics, and most people, girls as well as boys, have developed some interest in physical fitness. If there's a special sport you enjoy, see if it could be converted into an enjoyable dating activity. Tennis, bowling, volleyball, swimming, and even jogging all work well as activities two people can enjoy together.

Linda, a high school freshman, began to date Richard, a sophomore, in midwinter. At first they dated rather infrequently, about twice a month. Both were seeing other people at the time. However, as the months passed, the two grew closer, finding that they really enjoyed one another's company. They soon began to see each other exclusively. Linda and Richard began going out together at least three or four times a week in addition to speaking to each other on the telephone every evening. Before long they made it a point to see each other every day outside of school. The two spent a lot of time together with very little money to spend.

For a good deal of the time Linda and Richard just hung out. After school they'd go to the pizzeria, the candy store to play the pinball machines, or take long walks together. Sometimes, they'd do their homework together at one or the other's house. Occasionally when Richard had the money, they'd go to the movies. But before long it was clear that although they enjoyed each other's company, both were becoming bored with the relationship.

Linda began to think up new ways to add sparkle to their relationship. She took a long hard look at their lives and realized that many of the exciting or fun things they did were done by themselves or with other people. Both Linda and Richard were avid joggers. Each jogged a minimum of a mile every morning before school and got up a half hour earlier to do so. One day Linda suggested that they try jogging together. Joint jogging proved to be quite successful for Richard and Linda. They took turns jogging to one another's house, then once around the local park's reservoir, and back to either's house for breakfast. They'd then part, shower, and dress for school and later see each other for lunch in the school cafeteria. Their daily jogging date seemed to add quite a bit to their relationship.

*

Joe, a high school senior from New Jersey, had a similar experience with his girl friend, Sandy. Joe, who loved to hike, was an active member of a hiking and nature club which generally met on Saturday or Sunday afternoons. After a while when Sandy began to complain about the amount of time he spent away from her on weekends, Joe decided to take her along. Sandy loved the outdoors and soon became quite an able hiker. Before long she began mapping out special trails for them to take.

*

If you live near a beach or a lake, swimming dates are a great idea for the summer. If you like to swim year round, many towns have municipal swimming pools open to the public at a low cost. Do a bit of research and find out what's available and free in your area. Often there are parks, zoos, and a variety of interesting stores. Don and Joan, both high school sophomores who live in New York City, love animals and spend a good deal of time at the Bronx Zoo. They've taken all the zoo tours available, and they keep track of changing exhibits.

A picnic in a scenic corner of a park can make a wonderful date. A ride along a bicycle path can be fun as well. Shopping trips are not necessarily limited to walking up and down the aisles of a large supermarket. Many young couples enjoy visiting shopping malls in their area. Record and poster stores, jewelry shops, and sporting goods stores can be especially enjoyable.

If you don't live in a large urban center where numerous theatrical productions are available, see if any local theater groups in your town do special productions in the summer. Churches and synagogues often have groups that put on plays for which the tickets are fairly inexpensive.

There's always the old standard date of taking someone to the movies. People have used this successful dating activity for years, and as most people enjoy cinema, it usually goes over well. Just make sure the film you choose is one that both you and your date will enjoy, and be certain as well that your date hasn't already seen the picture.

As the cost of movie tickets has skyrocketed in recent years, check to see if there's a discount cinema in your area. At different times during the year these discount houses may offer film festivals featuring the work of one special artist where you can purchase strips of tickets at even lower prices. If you live near a college you may really be in luck. Often colleges and universities offer good films for their students at a fraction of what it would cost to go to a standard movie. Usually these films are open to the public, so be on the lookout for them.

Watch the local papers for festivals and bazaars. Many large cities offer ethnic food fairs during which whole city streets are blocked off, as vendors provide passersby with delicious, exotic morsels to munch on. Many times music is also provided resulting in a lively festive atmosphere. The total experience makes for an exciting date. Usually the only charge is for food. In smaller locales, churches and municipal groups often sponsor bazaars and fairs that are open to the public.

Boating dates are great for the summer, just as sledding and sleigh-riding are fun in the winter. If you live in New York City, you and your date can take a ride on the Staten Island ferry. If your home is in a smaller town, you might want to rent a paddle boat at a local lake. For some sledding fun in the winter all you need is a sled, a snow-covered hill, and a lot of courage.

Sleigh-riding through snow-covered country can be a beautiful, romantic experience, but renting a sleigh and driver for only two people can be quite expensive. Many livery stables do offer lower rates during their off-season. If even the lowered rates are still too high for you, consider inviting along one or two other couples and splitting the expenses. If you live in an area where it never snows, try to find a beach where you and your date can take part in a volleyball game, or a park equipped with tennis, paddle ball, or squash courts.

Ice skating dates can be great fun, especially if you find a municipal rink where you can skate at a low cost, or better still a well-frozen lake near your home. Roller skating dates, too, tend to lend themselves to laughter and antics, so it's often fun to invite another couple to join you.

Do you have a hobby like doing yoga or making stained glass ornaments? Try sharing the experience with your date sometime. Not only will your date have the opportunity to see something you really enjoy and spend time on, he or she will also be introduced to something new. Practicing yoga, attending a lecture on the subject, or teaching your date to meditate are all free. Stained glass work and photography can be expensive, but when introducing your date to your hobby for the first time, it shouldn't cost you much more than you usually spend. If your date really takes to your hobby and wishes to do it with you often, it's likely that he or she will supply his or her own equipment and materials.

That's what happened after John and Tina began to go steady. John, a high school senior, had become interested in photography when he first entered high school and joined the school's photography club. He soon became quite adept at it and won several contests sponsored by local newspapers for high school students.

John decided to enter a new competition for the best animal photograph of the year at about the same time he and Tina began going steady. Between his school work, his afternoon job at the drugstore, and his determination to win the contest, John had little time left to date. Tina, who adored animals and hoped to one day become a veterinarian, convinced John to take her along as he visited the neighboring farm lands to scout for good material. Tina proved to have a skillful eye for determining what would produce an excellent shot. John was quite awed by what appeared to be her almost natural knack for pointing out angles and details.

Tina used John's equipment to take a number of shots. She was so pleased with the results that she soon used the money she had earned babysitting to purchase her own camera and equipment. Photography became a part of John and Tina's dating routine, and the two continued to take pictures together long after the photography contest was over.

Museums often provide an enjoyable dating experience, but unfortunately the better-known ones are usually only located in large urban areas. Try checking out restorations of houses or historical sites.

Bone up on what local organizations and civic groups have to offer. Churches and synagogues often sponsor dances, picnics, and other activities for young people. Many municipalities sponsor Fourth of July and Labor Day weekend fireworks that are quite spectacular. If you live near a shore resort, fireworks may be offered even more often during the tourist season. In most places, these displays are free of charge.

Local libraries also offer special programs for young adults. If you and your date are avid readers, a library book discussion group may supply you both with quite a bit to talk about afterwards. Susan and Mark, two high school juniors who had been dating each other for about four months, attended a young adult Saturday afternoon workshop at their local library. They created slogans and designs which were then printed on T-shirts. They enjoyed themselves so much that they promised each other they would return the next time the workshop was offered.

Design your own personalized walking tour. Pick a new area you and your date can have fun exploring. Try to stay away from the streets you use every day, they'll be too familiar. At the same time, avoid overly deserted areas for the sake of safety.

After you've been going with someone for a while, you and your date may find it rewarding to do something for someone else. Bake a cake or make a wood carving for one of your grandmothers or aunts and deliver it together. Karen and Bob decided to volunteer some time together at their local hospital. Although they were placed in different wards, they met on their breaks and always went out for ice cream afterwards.

If you live in the country and can afford to rent horses for an hour or two, horseback riding is a great dating activity that allows you to enjoy the scenery as well as each other's company. Unfortunately, horses tend to be scarce in the city, and the cost of renting them is often prohibitive.

Once you've been seeing someone for a while, it can be fun to learn something new together. Search for unusual materials and create a terrarium. Check out a few geology books from your local library and try rock collecting. Make a decoupage wastepaper basket for your room or a sports collage mural for your wall. Create crazy balloon animals or decorate Easter eggs together and give them to your younger brothers and sisters or deliver them to the nearest hospital. Invite one or two other couples over to either of your houses and practice the latest disco dances.

Although it's been said that the best things in life are free, there are many people who believe the contrary. Even if you pick out an activity that is generally free, there are hidden costs involved—paying for the gas it took to drive to the high school dance or the refreshments you bought after that long walk through the park on a hot summer day. The library T-shirt printing workshop that Mark and Susan attended was free, but each participant still had to supply his or her own shirt.

Traditionally the boy was expected to pay for all the expenses incurred on a date. However in recent times there has been a change in the way some people view how dating costs should be taken care of. Some young men object to paying for both people on a date. They stress that if they are going to school at the time and not working or only working part-time, dating expenses can take a severe bite out of their allowances. As Dick, a high school junior from New York, put it, "Sandy and I have been going steady for about six months now. She's a beautiful girl and I'm crazy about her, but if she didn't pay her own way, I couldn't afford to go with her. We see each other every day and that almost always involves a Coke, a slice of pizza, an ice cream cone, or something. On Saturday night we try to go out on a special date to a movie or The Ice Palace, our favorite disco. Sandy loves live rock music, but do you have any idea what tickets to a rock concert go for today? I mean everything is just too high."

Larry, a high school sophomore from Washington, D.C., feels similarly: "I'll pay for a girl on maybe the first or second date, but after that forget it. And I'm not ashamed to bring the issue up either. Last year I met a girl at one of the school dances that I went with for a couple of months. She had a steady babysitting job on Saturday and Sunday afternoons plus an allowance that was far more generous than mine. It would have been ridiculous for me to pay for her on our dates. In fact, at times I thought she ought to pay for me. Of course, I never brought that up. I may be bold, but I'm not crazy."

When asked how she felt about going Dutch treat on a date, Kathy, a high school senior from Colorado, replied,

> I always pay for myself on dates. I work in a flower shop after school plus I get an allowance from my parents, so the financial resources are available to me. Besides that, it's important to me as a person to do so. I'm not a piece of property that a guy can buy for a slice of pizza and a Coke. When I was younger I used to let guys pay for me, but I never really felt free on my dates. If we went to a restaurant I always felt I had to order the cheapest thing on the menu, because after all it wasn't my own money. If my date asked me if I wanted dessert, I'd automatically say no. Even if I was dying for a hot fudge sundae, I'd make up some excuse about having to watch my weight —of course, the trouble with that one was that I was always naturally slender. Besides, those traditional dates weren't always so free. I went out with a lot of fast guys who insisted on spending money on me and later expected me to pay them back in the back seat of a car. It was awful; I hardly knew some of them. It's true that you don't have to go along with their demands, but if you pay your own way I truly believe that you don't owe anybody a thing. It changes the whole thing from obligation to choice.

Mary, a close friend of Kathy, also believes in paying for her own expenses on dates. According to Mary, "It really puts the two people on an equal footing. If a boy pays for me, I feel I have to go where he wants and do whatever he wants to do. After all, it's his money, so if he wants to go to a disco and I'd prefer a movie that night, I'll give in and go dancing. When you go Dutch you are free to suggest any activity at all. You never have to be afraid you'll embarrass the boy by bringing up something that he can't afford. I feel that by paying for myself on a date, I'm buying my freedom and the right to be myself."

Some teens feel quite differently about the issue. They are adamantly opposed to splitting dating expenses. When asked if she would be willing to pay her own way on a date, Cindy, a vivacious cheerleader, said, "I'd have to be crazy to go along with something like that. If any guy doesn't think I'm worth paying for, then he can just take out somebody else and take advantage of her by handing her half the bill. After all, I'm a lady and I have a right to be paid for. It's one of the advantages of being a girl and I feel that if a guy can't afford to pay for me on a date, then he can't afford to go out with me period."

Pam, a high school junior from Tennessee, had this to say about going Dutch treat: "I generally allow the young man to pay for me. I view it as common courtesy and don't believe it puts me under any strain or obligation. I always speak my own mind on a date; I think this makes me more of an individual and therefore a more desirable date. If a boy asks me where I'd like to go on our date, I have no hesitation about making my opinion known. After all, if he didn't want to please me, he wouldn't have asked me. I have never felt I had to go further with a boy on a date than I wanted to just because he paid the bill. If I felt that way I'd never go out at all. If a boy wants to kiss me and I don't want to, I simply won't allow it. And I don't care how much popcorn he bought me at the movies, that's not going to make me feel any differently."

Adam, a high school junior from New Jersey, believes that the male should take care of most of the dating expenses. He said, "Grace and I have been going steady for little more than a year now. I usually pay for our dates, and I don't mind doing so. It makes me feel good to take care of Grace in that way, and I know she appreciates it. Although I make certain that she has a voice in whatever activities we select, Grace has never been one to take advantage by selecting something outrageously expensive that would leave me broke for a month. Grace is terrific at doing special little extras to let me know she cares. She knitted me two sweaters, and last summer she surprised me by buying tickets to a rock concert I especially wanted to go to. She also took me out on my birthday and insisted on paying for the entire evening. It was her way of giving me a present. I know Grace is fabulous—she doesn't need to pay her own way on our dates to prove she's a worthwhile human being."

As is apparent from these interviews, there's quite a bit of current controversy over who should foot the dating bill. All these young people made valid points worth thinking about. Perhaps it is most important to remain flexible and evaluate each situation individually. In some situations you may feel you should pay, while at other times the opposite may be true. It's a very personal question, one you should not react blindly to out of habit. Be open, be free, and make sure you enjoy yourself, no matter who pays.

CHAPTER 

Rejection: How to Handle It

REJECT: 1. throw away as useless; discard
2. refuse to accept; decline
3. refuse to grant; deny—n. an imperfect article.

—*The New American Webster Handy College Dictionary*

To be rejected is one of the most painful experiences we may be forced to deal with in life. Rejection can occur on many levels, and at one time or another it happens to everyone.

Rejection can take different forms. You might not have done as well as you hoped to at the basketball tryouts and you were not chosen for the team. You might not have made the cheerleading squad or got the part you auditioned for in the school play last year. Perhaps you were turned down for an after school job you desperately wanted and needed or you might have been denied admission to the college of your choice.

It always hurts to hear you are not wanted, and the pain it brings varies with how much you desired the goal. Harold, a high school junior, wrote poetry which had been much admired by his family, friends, and English teachers. Writing poetry never meant very much to Harold. It was something that he did well with very little effort. Others might struggle over composing a beautiful sonnet, but to Harold it came easily. The things that mattered most to Harold in his life were playing basketball and his girl friend Marie. Harold's coach had always found it amusing that Harold had written some of his best poetry on the noisy bus rides to basketball games at other schools.

One winter during a parent-teacher conference at his school, Harold's English teacher told his mother about a state-wide poetry contest for high school students which she felt Harold should enter. When Harold's mother approached him regarding the contest, Harold said he really didn't care very much about it. He handed her a stack of his poems and told her to enter whatever she wished.

Harold's mother and his English teacher met several times after school to go through Harold's work. They selected those poems they thought were best representative of Harold's talent. The English teacher asked the opinion of other faculty members as well. Finally, Harold's mother and teacher selected two poems they believed to be genuinely outstanding. They felt certain that one of these entries would win the contest. Both anxiously awaited the judges' decision.

Unfortunately, the contest judges did not share Harold's mother and English teacher's evaluation of his work. Not only did Harold's poems not take first prize, neither received as much as an honorable mention. Harold's mother felt terrible about the contest results. She tried to break the news to Harold gently, as she was certain he would be terribly hurt and disappointed over the matter. She was astonished when Harold told her the contest outcome meant nothing to him. He hadn't been interested in the contest from the very beginning, and he reminded her that he hadn't even cared about which of his poems were chosen for entry. He assured his mother that he had only participated in the contest at all to please her.

Harold's mother felt certain her son was lying about the contest to hide his bruised ego. She said no more about the matter, as she didn't wish to dwell on a rejection which she believed must have been very painful to her child.

Although few people believed him, Harold was telling the truth. Other students at school would tell him how sorry they were that he didn't win the contest, and although they were sincere, Harold could not take them seriously. He had always taken very little interest in his writing ability and showed even less concern over the student competition.

Harold felt undaunted by the entire incident. Everything that was important to him in his world was intact and going well. He was self-assured and untouched by rejection at this point in his life. However, four months later, when his girl friend Marie left him for a college football player, he thought he was going to die.

Actually it all happened over the summer. Marie, the girl Harold had been going steadily with for over two years, got a job as a junior counselor at a sleep-away camp in the mountains. At the urging of her parents, Marie informed Harold that she was going to date other boys while she was away. She told Harold that she cared for him a great deal, but felt it was best that way since Marie firmly believed they were too young to get serious. However, Harold felt genuinely in love with Marie. He had felt that way from the first day he saw her three years before, brilliantly arguing her point at a debating club match. He couldn't prevent Marie from doing whatever she felt was right for her, but Harold felt no desire to see other girls and secretly hoped Marie wouldn't find anyone she liked at the camp.

That was not how things turned out. Marie was only at camp a week when she met Jerry, a college sophomore who played football for his school. He was working in the camp's athletic program as a senior counselor. Jerry was quite taken with Marie and asked her out. The two began seeing each other almost every night after work, and their relationship began to grow. By the time Marie returned to her hometown at summer's end, she and Jerry were going steady. Marie claimed to be deeply in love for the first time in her life and had no interest in seeing anyone else.

Harold could not understand how all this had happened in less than two months. It was true that Marie had stopped answering his daily letters after about a week and a half, but all the while Harold kept trying to convince himself that Marie was probably just too busy with her camp duties to answer her correspondence. At times he even tried to tell himself that Marie's letters were just lost or delayed in the mail, and that they would eventually find their way to his mailbox.

Of course, no further letters ever came. When Harold tried to call Marie once she had returned from camp, one of her three sisters always managed to tell him that she wasn't in. Harold finally had an opportunity to confront Marie at her locker on the second day of school. But when he saw Jerry's ring on a chain around her neck, he felt as though he already knew the whole story.

Marie was quite curt with her old boyfriend. She quickly and cruelly informed Harold that she was now going with a mature man who was very special to her. She told him that she and Jerry were quite serious about each other, and that Harold ought to start getting over her. When Harold reminded Marie that only a few months ago she had told him she felt she was too young to become involved in a serious relationship, Marie refused to listen any further. She excused herself and, with a toss of her head, quickly walked away.

Harold was shocked by what he regarded as Marie's brutality. He felt completely out of control. Marie hadn't given him an adequate explanation of why she had abandoned him for someone else. She had refused to discuss the issue with him any further, and this made Harold feel as if he were simply a victim of Marie's whims. In many ways, he was right.

It took a good deal of time before Harold began to feel better about Marie. He didn't start dating immediately. He had given his care and affection freely to Marie, and she had taken it all for granted. He wondered what would prevent the same thing from happening to him again, and he wasn't anxious to expose himself to this possibility.

During this period, Harold was forced to deal with many doubts. His self-confidence was shaken and he began to wonder about himself. Why didn't Marie love him any more? What did Jerry possess that he lacked? How could their relationship have meant so little to Marie? Was he inadquate as a person?

Such feelings frequently accompany the breakup of a relationship. This is especially true when the decision to dissolve the relationship is not mutual. It is difficult to separate the end of a love relationship from our feelings about our own self-worth. However, in reality there is no connection. The fact that Marie did not wish to date Harold now did not in any way change what Harold was. He was still a kind, intelligent, interesting human being, and the fact that Marie was no longer with him did not make him any the less so.

Although their relationship still worked for Harold, it was no longer right for Marie. At one point during the breakup Harold simply thought Marie was immature. It is difficult to know exactly what went on in Marie's mind, but perhaps she did not act as maturely as possible. She was impressed by the fact that Jerry was a college man and a football player, and was drawn to Jerry by superficialities. In any event, it was Marie's right to go with whomever she pleased and Harold's responsibility to himself to react to the rejection constructively.

Harold had done the correct thing in confronting Marie directly about his predicament. It is impossible to react to a situation in a positive manner unless you know exactly what that situation entails. With Marie refusing even to speak to him on the telephone, Harold wasn't really certain where he stood.

After finally speaking with Marie and learning that there was very little possibility of resuming their status as a couple, Harold had to accept that his relationship with Marie was over. As Harold still had feelings for her, this period was bound to be painful for him. During this time it was essential that Harold remember that there was nothing wrong with him personally. What was right for Marie once was no longer right for her now.

There's an old folk saying that goes something like, "The best way to fall out of love is to fall in love." It certainly might not be the best idea to run out and attempt to fall head over heels in love with the next person you meet, but it is a good idea to get out of the house and meet new people once an old relationship has ended. Harold waited many months before he even tried to go out with anyone else. In his hurt and anger, Harold refused to go to any school dances or church socials. He even stopped going out with his friends after school or on Friday nights, and he shunned all events where he could have met new girls.

Harold spent a good deal of time brooding over his

loss. Marie was no longer just an ordinary girl who had wanted to end a relationship. In his mind she had become a cruel and vicious tyrant who had unjustly wronged him. Harold relived every unkindness Marie had ever shown him in all the time he knew her. He thought of practically nothing else, and every day incidents were blown out of proportion. Harold actually caused himself a great deal of unnecessary pain. He would have been much better off if he had acknowledged that losing Marie hurt and then went on to form new relationships.

Going on isn't always easy, especially if you've just left a very intense relationship. Mike, a college freshman, broke up with his girl friend Betsy, a high school senior, a few months after entering college. It wasn't that he didn't care for Betsy any longer. He simply found that he had more in common with college girls. Also, Mike's school was about eighty miles away from his hometown where Betsy lived. A busy academic schedule kept him from returning home on weekends as often as he had hoped to, and their long-distance relationship became increasingly difficult to maintain.

Betsy was very hurt by Mike's decision to end their relationship. She had been willing to visit him at college every weekend, but Mike always seemed too busy with his studies to entertain her once she arrived. Besides, bus fare to his school was quite costly.

Betsy's reaction differed greatly from Harold's when Mike told her it was over between them. She didn't try to change Mike's mind. The instant she heard the news she reasoned, "Well, if that's what he wants, that's what he'll get." Yet that night Betsy cried herself to sleep, and for the next two weeks she spent a good deal of time on the telephone with her two best friends discussing her predicament. For a short time, she even took to treating herself to hot fudge sundaes after school.

Betsy was determined not to spend her time pining away for Mike. Almost immediately, she immersed herself in a series of activities through which she hoped to meet new boys. She began going to school dances, parties, and church socials on a regular basis. However, things did not go as smoothly as she had planned. It was true that Betsy did meet a great number of new boys, many of whom asked her out for dates. But Betsy simply didn't feel very attracted to any of them. In fact, it was during this period that Betsy became exceedingly particular about whom she dated. She found that one boy was too thin, another overweight, and still another boring.

Before long, the problem became apparent to Betsy: She had been comparing every boy she met to her old boyfriend Mike. Mike and Betsy had enjoyed a long relationship, one in which they had already worked out all the uneasiness and problems associated with beginnings. They had learned how to be comfortable with one another. Now Betsy had to learn not to expect this comforting familiarity with every new boy she went out with. She soon adjusted well to her new situation and began to once again enjoy dating. This time she took care not to rush immediately into an exclusive relationship. She dated a number of boys for several months before selecting a steady dating partner.

Though the unwanted breakup of a long dating relationship is a very painful form of rejection, lesser rejections in the area of romance carry their sting as well. "Cupid's Follies" is an annual girl-ask-boy St. Valentine's Day dance given at a south New Jersey high school. It's considered the event of the year, and weeks in advance many of the girls go on diets and buy new outfits. Lana, a high school student who did not do very much dating and had never gone to Cupid's Follies, was determined to attend the dance at least one time before she graduated.

Being that Lana was already a junior, she reasoned that she didn't have many opportunities left to her. She had never asked a boy out on a date before and even the thought of it terrified her. She discussed the situation with her friends, but none of them was very helpful. It seems that all Lana's friends had only very limited dating experience, and none was willing to risk asking a boy to Cupid's Follies that year.

Lana decided to approach this task in her usual organized manner. First she made a list of five boys whom she thought suitable to escort her to Cupid's Follies. She listed them according to preference, the most desirable boy heading the list. She didn't feel sufficiently brave to approach any of the boys face to face, so she decided to call. To make certain she didn't lose her nerve or unintentionally scramble her own message, she wrote down exactly what she planned to say in advance of the phone call.

Armed with all her courage and an ice cream soda, Lana dialed the first boy's number. Lana said hello, blurted out her message, and then waited with hotly flushed cheeks for a reply. The boy was polite when he told Lana that he had already been asked to Cupid's Follies by another girl. The same thing was true when Lana tried the second and third boys. The fourth boy told Lana that he was already dating someone steadily, and the fifth informed her in a very kind way that he didn't feel they were right for one another.

At first Lana felt devastated by the entire experience. She couldn't believe that after asking five boys, she had still been unable to secure a date for the dance. She felt depressed and was just about ready to give up on the whole idea, when one of her close girl friends came to her aid with some clear thinking. Her friend explained that just because five boys weren't able to take Lana to the dance that didn't change the fact that Lana was a wonderful person. There might be five hundred other boys who would have loved to escort her. Lana's friend agreed that it must be difficult to handle five rejections in a row, but stressed that that didn't mean that everything was over for Lana.

Lana decided that her friend was right. She wanted to go to Cupid's Follies and was determined to go to the dance with someone whose company she'd enjoy. She realized that just because five boys out of all the boys she knew were unable to take her, that didn't mean that her evening had to be spoiled. Lana continued her quest for a date to the St. Valentine's Day dance. The very next boy she asked said he'd be delighted to go to Cupid's Follies with her.

Sometimes even less meaningful rejections can cause pain. It is difficult to go to a dance in a good mood wearing a new outfit and looking your most beautiful only to find that no one asks you to dance. It can especially hurt when all your friends are gracefully spinning away on the dance floor.

It isn't necessary to stand there and simply accept the rejection. There are alternatives available to you. If no one is asking you to dance, try talking to someone. It is preferable to speak with someone of the opposite sex, but if there's no such person available and you don't have the courage to approach someone new, just walk over to someone you know and begin a conversation. It will make you feel more secure and less alone, and before you know it, you'll begin to relax.

Don't be afraid to take the initiative in romantic situations. Because people fear rejection, they often hesitate to take important steps that would make real differences. Rejection in and of itself means nothing; the important thing is how you react to the rejection. If you should be rejected, it is important not to attribute too much authority and power to the individual who rejected you. No one but you can determine your worth. Often the rejection has very little to do with you. This is especially true when you are approaching someone for the first time at a dance or asking someone out for an initial date. If the person doesn't know you, he or she truly has little valid reason for rejecting you.

A lot depends on how the person felt about him- or herself at the time. It is always possible that the person had to deal with problems regarding school, friends, or parents. It is also possible that the individual was just entering or ending another relationship or was currently deeply involved with someone else.

You also must realize that no one person is going to have all the qualities desired by everyone. Most people have preconceived notions of what physical characteristics they look for in dating partners. Some like tall, dark types while others prefer blue-eyed blondes. If you don't fit one individual's stereotype, it doesn't mean you are unattractive. Marian, a green-eyed blond from Montclair, New Jersey, had been anxious to go out with Larry, a senior from her school, for a number of months.

Marian did everything in her power to make Larry notice her. At first she always managed to get a seat near his in the cafeteria or just happen to pass by his locker as he was opening it at the end of the day. She memorized his schedule of classes and tried to be stationed at each particular hallway he'd have to walk through.

Marian started endless conversations with Larry, read up on the things that interested him, and flattered him continuously. Her efforts did not end with the school day. When she and her two best girl friends went for long bike rides on Saturday mornings, they inevitably ended up parking their bikes on Larry's lawn where they stopped to rest. If the sight of the girls on the lawn didn't bring Larry out of the house or if he didn't happen to be near a window when they arrived, Marian simply rang his bell and asked for a glass of water.

Several months of such diligent effort on Marian's part brought no real results. Larry was nice enough to her—he was always sweet and polite and even managed to laugh at some of Marian's not-so-funny jokes. Still, he never asked her for a date. Worn out by all this hard work, Marian decided to try to get some inside information on what was happening. One of Marian's best friends was dating a boy who was quite close to Larry. Marian and her friend decided to send this young man on the mission of finding out what was the matter. He soon reported back to the girls that although Larry liked Marian very much as a person, he did not find her physically attractive enough to ask out on a date.

The news shocked everyone involved. Marian was generally considered a beauty by most of the boys at school. She could have had dates with many different boys, but she had taken a liking to Larry and wanted very much to date him. When Larry's friend expressed surprise at what Larry said, Larry answered that, although some people considered Marian to be an extremely attractive young woman, she simply wasn't his type. He went on to explain that he liked small, dark-haired, pixie-type girls. Girls with black hair and sparkling brown eyes held a special appeal for him. Marian was the exact opposite of everything Larry found physically appealing in a girl; apparently physical attractiveness meant a great deal to Larry. The fact that Marian wasn't Larry's type did not make her a less attractive girl or a less desirable dating partner.

There are a number of ways to help combat rejection. It is always important to be aware of incidents in which the odds are so against you that you are involved in an almost impossible situation. This does not mean quitting and running away from an unpleasant incident. It means avoiding negative predicaments in which the rejection is likely to compound itself. Marian dedicated several months to trying to get Larry to ask her out. Her efforts caused her a great deal of pain when Larry ignored all her advances. She kept it up for several months, when she should have stopped after a few weeks. Of course, there was always the possibility that Larry was shy and needed some encouragement, but if that were the case, it certainly should not have taken such a massive effort on Marian's part. A direct confrontation should not have been necessary. Marian should have realized the situation through Larry's actions.

Nothing soothes the rejected soul like a bit of pampering. Be good to yourself—someone else hasn't been very kind to you lately. Don't unjustly blame yourself for something out of your control. Now is the time to buy that new album, order that magazine subscription, or splurge on that dress you've been wanting. If you love ice cream or chocolate chip cookies, treat yourself (but in moderation). Make something positive happen to you. You might not be able to manufacture a budding romance overnight, but you may be able to raise your average in history, and that can also make you feel better. When you do feel more positive about yourself, go out and tackle a new romantic quest. Give it enough time and it will happen to you.

CHAPTER 

Teen Marriage—Heaven or Heartache?

Marriage in our society is often thought of as the end result of love. As an institution, marriage has been greatly romanticized. Little girls are given dolls in beautiful white bridal gowns to play with. In their fantasies, the dolls represent themselves. Many hours of their young lives are spent dreaming about the day they will walk down the aisle.

Dreams about beautiful bridal gowns, white wedding doves, and diamond rings are often nothing more than dreams. After the ceremony, two people are expected to live happily together for the rest of their lives. This is often not an easy task, and it can be especially difficult when the two people involved are teenagers.

Statistics on the success of teen marriages suggest little to recommend it. There are numerous reasons to support the figures. The teen years are a time of growth and exploration. It is your chance to find out who you really are as an individual. During this period most young people are fortunate enough to live with minimal responsibilities. Their parents pay for all their major expenses and often they only need enough money to pay for the luxuries they want.

The teen years are also a time for learning about love. The dates you go on now, the painful crushes you suffer through, the rejections you learn to deal with, and the problems within a love relationship which you learn to work through, are all valuable and important experiences which help to prepare you for later life.

Still, we all tend to associate love with marriage. Even though you may be a teenager, when you are deeply in love with someone, marriage may appear to be the right alternative. That's exactly what happened to Cindy and Bob, two young people from New Jersey. Bob, who had never been a very good student, left high school at the age of seventeen to work as a mechanic in his father's garage. Bob loved automobiles; in fact, cars were the major passion of his life. As a young boy he had spent Saturdays and afternoons after school watching his father work at the garage. He was well liked by the mechanics who were employed there, and after a time the men actually came to look forward to the little boy's visits. Bob was an only child, and it had been his parents' wish that he would take over the garage when his father retired. Bob's parents had hoped he would finish school, but when he decided to quit and work full time as a mechanic, they were not terribly disappointed at his decision.

Cindy, an adorable sixteen year old, had been going with Bob since she was fourteen. She had a lot in common with her boyfriend, and as a couple they got along quite well. However, there was one marked difference between Bob and Cindy: Cindy was an exceptional student. It wasn't that Cindy was a particularly good math student or English scholar, she just seemed to excel in everything she tried. That year she had won the Science Award at school for creating the most inventive science project, while at the same time being at the top of her home economics class. Cindy was simply a brilliant young woman with great academic promise.

Bob felt he knew exactly what he wanted out of life—to take over the garage and marry Cindy. Cindy's goals could not be defined as simplistically. It was as if Cindy wanted a taste of everything. She definitely knew she wanted to marry one day, and right then she felt certain Bob would be her husband. Cindy often said, "I know I want to have at least six kids, so I won't ever have to worry about being lonely.

But Cindy had other dreams as well. Most of the time she thought she wanted to be a biochemist, but over the course of a few months Cindy's career goals would vary. At different times she thought of being a botanist, a model, or even a psychologist. Cindy had a great deal of confidence in herself. She felt she could be anything she wished to be.

A few months after Bob quit school, his feelings

about himself began to change. He felt more grown up and reasoned that this was due to the increased responsibility he had taken on at the garage. He was tired of living at home with his parents. He loved his mother and father, but he felt it was time he had a home of his own, and he wanted Cindy to share that home with him. Cindy and Bob had discussed marriage during the course of their relationship. It was something they were going to do when they grew up. Now it seemed as though Bob had grown up very suddenly.

When he spoke to Cindy about getting married right away, Cindy had difficulty believing that all this was happening to her. At first she put down the idea, saying to Bob, "Don't be ridiculous, we're just kids." But secretly the thought delighted her. Now all her other dreams were pushed aside as she fantasized about "Cindy the homemaker." Cindy's mother didn't work; she had been a housewife most of her life and loved it. Cindy soon began to believe that she'd enjoy the life her mother had had, but reasoned that she might also become an astronaut once her six future children were all in school.

In any case, although Cindy thought of nothing else, she still wasn't ready to accept the idea completely.

Whenever Bob brought up the prospect of an immediate marriage, Cindy quickly changed the subject. However, all the while she secretly bought bride's magazines and designed bridal gowns as an independent project for her art class.

Bob soon grew impatient with Cindy's evasiveness. He thought that because she hadn't rushed to marry him, perhaps she really didn't love him. He felt a bit hurt and decided to take a firmer stand on the issue. Bob decided to do so with a very special gift for Cindy. Christmas was only a few weeks away, and Bob was determined to present Cindy with a diamond engagement ring on Christmas Eve. If Cindy would not accept the ring, Bob reasoned that it would be best if they broke up. Bob did feel fairly secure that no girl—including Cindy—would pass up a diamond.

He was right. Over the holidays, when he handed Cindy the small black velvet box which held the ring, her face lit up. It was as if she already knew what it contained. She opened the box, slipped the ring on her finger, and, as hot tears streamed down her face, exclaimed "Yes, yes." Bob hadn't even needed to ask her to marry him again.

At the time Cindy was quite impressed with her new piece of jewelry. She had never owned a diamond before, but had dreamed of wearing a diamond engagement ring since she was a very young girl. She and her girl friends had looked at pictures of diamond rings in magazines and had discussed the size, shape, and color of the various stones that appealed to them. Now she was the first among her friends to own one, and this reality sent her dreams about marriage soaring to new heights.

The parents of each took the news very differently. After being informed of their son's engagement to Cindy, Bob's parents embraced their daughter-in-law to be and welcomed her into the family. When Cindy told her parents, her mother pulled the ring off her finger, while her father slapped her across the face and sent her to her room. Cindy was outraged at such treatment. At this point in her life she believed her parents to be cruel, insensitive individuals who were only interested in seeing Cindy achieve at school and cared little for her personal happiness.

When Cindy discussed the matter with them later, they remained adamant. They firmly believed that their daughter was far too young to even consider marriage and that it was imperative that she finish her education and establish a career before selecting a husband. They also insinuated that they weren't delighted with the fact that Bob had left school.

Cindy related her parents' sentiments to Bob, but he was determined not to allow that to interfere with their plans. The two decided to go ahead with the marriage. They soon learned, however, that this was not as easy as they had hoped. Cindy was only sixteen years old and could not marry in her state without her parents' consent.

Cindy once again approached her parents about her impending marriage, but this time she decided to deliver a painful ultimatum to them. She told her parents that if they didn't give their consent to her marriage, she and Bob would go off and live together without the benefit of a legal bond. She added that they would immediately start a family.

Cindy's parents were both shocked and alarmed by her threat. They believed the alternative Cindy presented to be highly immoral and decided they'd rather see their daughter married than living the kind of life she described. Reluctantly, they gave their consent to the marriage.

Cindy and Bob had a small wedding at their church. Cindy's parents felt so strongly against this union, they thought it would be hypocritical to host a lavish party in celebration. Finding a place to live proved to be difficult for the young couple. Cindy didn't work and Bob didn't earn very much money, so the number of apartments available to them was severely limited. After an unproductive and exhaustive search, they settled on renting the apartment above the garage where Bob worked. It was very convenient to Bob's employment, and Bob's parents owned the building, so Bob and Cindy were charged a rent they could afford.

In the fall Cindy dropped out of school during the day and enrolled in the evening adult education program offered by her school. Cindy didn't know it at the time of her wedding, but married students were not permitted to attend classes during the day. In addition to everything else, this change called for a tremendous adjustment on Cindy's part. She greatly missed her friends and teachers, and the after school activities that had become so much a part of her everyday world. As most of the evening students worked during the day, Cindy found that she didn't have very much in common with them. She also soon learned that few extracurricula activities were offered at the night school. The students there were generally considered too busy to take advantage of them.

Cindy didn't drive, and her new apartment was quite a distance from the school. Since public transportation was scant in her area in the evening, Bob had to drive her to and from her classes. Since he was often quite tired after a long day at the garage, these journeys to Cindy's school placed an additional strain on Bob.

For the first few months of the marriage things went along well enough. Cindy and Bob felt as though they were playing house, and they both appeared to derive some satisfaction from their new situation. However, as time passed, seemingly small incidents began to eat away at both Bob and Cindy, causing a negative effect on their marriage.

Cindy began to feel very distant and isolated from her friends. It was as if she no longer had very much in common with the girls she had once been extremely close to. Their lives seemed to revolve around getting dates, going to parties, and making the cheerleading squad. Their mothers cooked for them, so whenever Cindy tried to tell one of them about a new budget recipe, she found they tried quickly to change the topic. Whenever she spoke to her friends about how difficult it was to live in a very confined space with another person, they seemed to almost ignore her problem and tell her instead that she was lucky to have something more than a boy friend. Cindy was free during the day, but her friends attended classes then. In the evenings she cooked dinner for Bob and attended school, so there was little recreational time to spend with her friends. Cindy soon began to feel as if a very vital part of her life had vanished.

There were other problems as well. When Cindy lived at home, all her material needs had been met by her parents. In addition, she was given an ample allowance for small luxuries. As a result, Cindy entered her marriage with very little budgeting experience. She had never handled home finances in her life and had no idea of how to shop for a bargain or balance a checkbook. After a short time, Cindy realized how little money she and Bob actually had to live on. For the first time in her life, Cindy was forced to live economically, and she felt very little inclination to be thrifty.

Cindy also felt that things were beginning to change between Bob and herself. She had always found it very romantic when Bob came to pick her up for a date all dressed and looking his best. She didn't find that washing out his socks and underwear gave her the same glamorous feeling. Bob was beginning to spend more and more time away from home, too. He frequently went out for beers with the other mechanics after work, leaving Cindy alone until well into the evening. On the weekends, Cindy often felt isolated and deserted when Bob left her alone all day while he worked on his car. Cindy complained that he had certainly been anxious enough to see her as often as possible when they were going out together—now he seemed to need a good deal of time to be by himself. This was a need Cindy had a great deal of trouble sympathizing with.

Cindy also began to feel increasingly alienated from her family. Her parents continued to express their anger and disappointment in their daughter every time they saw her. She had always felt that she had been her mother's favorite, but now she began to feel that her younger sister, Julie, was rapidly replacing her as the family star. Cindy felt that when she saw her mother, all her mother spoke of was how well Julie was doing in school or how Julie had just made the cheerleading squad or the color guard. It was Julie who went through the tryouts and won the singing lead in this year's school musical. It was Julie who was now dating Tom, an athletic, handsome senior whom Cindy had a crush on for several years. Before her marriage Cindy had tried to get Tom's attention, but he never asked her out. Now her mother informed Cindy that Tom was absolutely crazy about little Julie. Cindy felt her jealousy for Julie's freedom and luck reach a new height when Julie told Cindy that although Tom had asked her repeatedly to go steady, she continually refused, since she felt the relationship would be too confining.

All of a sudden Cindy felt as if everything were passing her by. For the first time she began to realize that it would be possible for her to spend the rest of her life cooking, cleaning, and tending to Bob's needs rather than her own. However, what Cindy considered self-sacrifice on her part didn't impress Bob in the least. He found himself quite dissatisfied with Cindy's role and often verbalized his feelings about it. In fact, at times Cindy thought he complained about everything she did. He was disappointed in her cooking skills and often criticized her for her lack of inventiveness and organization when it came to preparing meals. He resented having to chauffeur her to and from classes at night and couldn't understand why she wanted to finish school, since he had dropped out. Bob felt it was not fitting for a wife to have more education than her husband.

Bob argued that Cindy was becoming a nag, and

that she was trying to close him in too tightly. Cindy argued that she had given up everything important for Bob. Her marriage had alienated her from her family and friends, and now Bob seemed more interested in drinking beer with the boys than in spending time with her. She didn't want to quit school since it was now the only bright spot in her life.

However, under pressure from Bob, Cindy eventually did quit school. Soon after that she gave birth to a baby girl. After the birth of their child, the pressures brought to bear on the young couple became too great—Cindy left Bob and filed for a divorce.

Cindy went back to live with her parents. She wanted everything in her life to be as it was before she left, but unfortunately that was impossible. Cindy was now a mother. Her parents and sister tried to convince her that she was too young to be responsible for a baby and pleaded with her to put the child up for adoption. But Cindy loved her daughter and couldn't bear to part with her. As a result, both Cindy and her new daughter took up residence in her parents' home.

Cindy was able to attend school during the day once again, but was forced to spend almost all her time out of school caring for her child. Even though she was no longer living with Bob, Cindy found that she still had very little in common with her formerly close girl friends. She felt as if she had matured greatly because of her experience, and the differences in perception separated the girls.

Cindy also had trouble relating to the boys at school. They simply didn't seem to understand what she had been through. Many steered away from Cindy because they feared the responsibility of becoming involved with a young girl who had a small child to care for. In any case, since Cindy couldn't afford babysitters on her allowance, she had little opportunity to go out on dates.

Bob too experienced a great deal of pain in his separation from Cindy. He was deeply hurt over what had happened to him. He felt as if a moment ago he was a married man and now he was suddenly divorced and alone. He couldn't understand why Cindy felt she had to leave him. He thought he had provided Cindy with a good home and that the divorce had been entirely her fault. In his mind, Cindy was a poor homemaker, and he believed that was what destroyed the marriage. He reasoned that since his mother had found satisfaction staying at home and caring for a family, Cindy should do the same. He complained bitterly that he missed his little daughter and often said that he wanted to keep her with him. However, his mother was too old and sickly to care for a baby, and Bob saw no other way to provide for her care. As a result, he was only able to see his child on Sunday afternoons for a few hours.

Neither Cindy nor Bob were cruel or unreasonable people. They were simply two people who married too young and suffered the consequences of many teenage marriages. At sixteen and seventeen years of age, Bob and Cindy didn't have the maturity and experience to build a meaningful life together. They still were growing and changing—it was necessary for them to find themselves before they could find one another.

Both teenagers had unrealistic and romanticized notions about marriage. Bob felt that Cindy should be content with being the happy homemaker and nothing else, while Cindy unwisely believed that she could easily juggle the roles of homemaker, mother, and scholar at the same time. Both people missed the freedom that they should have been enjoying during their teen years.

Many people believe a marriage can be swiftly aborted by a divorce, but the repercussions of even a short marriage may go on for many years. Although Bob is not able to see his daughter as often as he would like, he is legally bound to contribute to her support until she is eighteen years of age. If Bob ever intends to remarry and establish another family, he will carry this financial burden into his new situation.

Even when a young couple appears to be adequately mature and well matched with one another, the odds against a teen marriage surviving can weigh heavily on the relationship. That's what happened to Eric and Greta, a young couple from Michigan.

Although Eric and Greta had dated continually through all of high school, they thought it was wise to wait until after they graduated to marry. They graduated in June and were married in August. The parents of both had been friends for many years and were delighted with the union, but they were also glad that their children had waited. Eric and Greta had a beautiful wedding in a quaint chapel a few miles from their hometown. Greta's parents provided a lovely reception for the couple at a nearby restaurant. After a short Florida honeymoon, the couple stayed with Greta's parents for the following few weeks.

Eric and Greta would be attending the same university in the fall. They had been fortunate that dormitory space for married students had been available at the college they chose. Since they'd be leaving for school in a few weeks, they felt no need to rent their own apartment for such a short period of time. Eric and Greta were both grateful to Greta's parents for putting them up.

Living with Greta's parents got their marriage off to an unusual start. Although the newly married couple shared Greta's bedroom, Greta's parents treated them as if they were brother and sister living in the same house. Greta's mother cooked all their meals, did their laundry, and even cleaned their room. When they went out at night, Greta's parents would gently warn the couple not to come home too late. Eric and Greta began to feel like overgrown children living in a doll's house. They were married, but they had not yet begun to deal with the normal stresses of adulthood and marriage.

When Eric and Greta left for college in September, the recognition of their new obligations and responsibilities made quite a forceful impact. In order to get married, both had agreed to take part-time jobs at school to help meet expenses. This proved to be very difficult for the new students. Greta found a convenient and interesting job at the college bookstore, but the salary was so low that she was forced to work many more hours than she had wanted to.

Eric was not nearly as lucky. After unsuccessfully looking for employment at school, he got a job waiting on tables in a restaurant in the local town, about five miles from campus. Eric worked evenings and was required to stay to clean up after the restaurant closed; he often did not return home until after 2 A.M. Local bus transportation stopped after midnight, so on late nights he either had to hitch a ride back to campus or walk the five miles. As winter set in the bitter cold made this especially difficult. To make matters worse, Eric often had to get up at 6 the next morning to attend early classes.

Greta and Eric had always loved being together, but now they were forced to spend many hours apart. Neither had ever worked before, and the adjustment to their new job situations was difficult for both of them. With the added stress of the demands stemming from school and marriage, the young couple found they were bickering more than ever before. At times, small differences mushroomed into heated arguments, and neither Eric nor Greta could understand why.

On Friday and Saturday nights the restaurant where Eric worked became a disco for the young college people in the area. Eric had to watch his classmates laugh, dance, drink beer, and have a good time. He couldn't join in the fun—it was his job to wait on them. Eric found himself resenting his job and resenting the marriage that forced him to be an outsider among his own peers.

Greta's job began to interfere with her marriage too, but in a very different way. A portion of Greta's work at the bookstore involved her taking book orders from the professors and making sure the proper texts were delivered to the correct shelves for the various classes. As an anthropology major, Greta took special relish in making certain the anthropology books were done with the greatest care. Mr. K., a tall, handsome, recently divorced anthropology teacher, was so impressed with the job being done that he decided to come down to the school bookstore to thank personally whoever was responsible. After complimenting the store manager, Mr. K. was introduced to Greta. Mr. K. took one look at Greta and asked her out to lunch.

Greta daydreamed about their lunch together for days after. Mr. K. had so impressed her. He spoke of all the recent trends in anthropology and how he was certain that Greta would go far in the field. He seemed to know everything and gave informative answers to all of Greta's questions. Greta thanked Mr. K. for lunch and then practically ran all the way home to tell Eric all about him.

Mr. K. came to visit Greta at the bookstore a number of times during the next few weeks. He often took her out for coffee or lunch. She was always happy to see him and was quite delighted that a professor had taken such an interest in her. At times he spoke to Greta about the popular archeological digs to foreign countries that he conducted for students during the summer months. He said that he hoped Greta would be able to sign up for a least one during her next few years at school. Greta then informed Mr. K. of her recent marriage and how it would be unthinkable for her to leave Eric over the summer to go on an archeological excavation. For the first time, Greta sharply realized how her marriage had limited the opportunities available to her.

After learning of Greta's marriage, Mr. K. began to see less and less of her. Greta wondered if this was simply a coincidence, or if Mr. K. had ever entertained romantic notions about her. She thrilled to the thought of dating someone like Mr. K. He was suave, sophisticated, and very knowledgeable. Greta thought that she'd rather be out with Mr. K. than with a movie star. She kept imagining what it would be like to go with him or even be married to him and attend faculty functions as his wife. It was exciting to talk with someone in her field. Eric didn't have the slightest interest in archaeology. She and Eric had married before they had discovered their individual interests and chosen their majors in college.

Greta quickly flushed thoughts about Mr. K. from her mind. She felt guilty even thinking about another man. At about the same time, Eric was beginning to deal with some potent feelings of guilt himself. Working at the disco, he saw many beautiful young women looking their best. A number of these girls had come to the disco hoping to meet new men. Although Eric was an employee there, several of the girls were quite forward with him and tried to engage him in conversations.

Judy, a tall, dark, sultry senior, made it a point of asking to be seated at one of Eric's tables every Friday night. After a few weeks she began to wait until closing time to drive Eric home.

Eric had mixed feelings about accepting the ride. He had never initiated any romantic moves toward Judy, and he tried to tell himself that she was nothing more than a friend. Still, he felt extremely attracted to her. Judy was three years older than Eric, and he began to think of her as an older woman. This perception of her somehow added to her appeal. Eric saw Judy as being witty, glamorous, and extremely attentive to him. She was always anxious to hear about whatever interested him.

Eric hardly ever had a chance to speak to Greta anymore. When he returned home at night, Greta was usually sound asleep. On most days she left for class or for her job at the bookstore before Eric woke up. Even when he did see her in the afternoons, they usually had very little to say to each other. It wasn't as if they were angry at one another. They were simply growing up, and somehow they were growing apart at the same time.

When Eric and Greta did have an opportunity to go out together, they often felt like misfits on campus. There were few married couples at the college. Most of the married students were housewives who went to classes during the day and then returned home to their husbands and children at night. Almost all the social activities at the university were geared toward single people. There were about four "singles mingles" a week and hardly ever any events scheduled for couples. The students even used the movies shown on campus as an opportunity to meet members of the opposite sex. Frequently, when Eric would get up during the film to buy a soda for Greta, another young man would try to jump into his seat and initiate a conversation with Greta.

Eric and Greta began to feel increasingly out of place. Even when they formed friendships with members of their own sex, they often felt like outsiders looking in. Greta began to feel envious of other young women students who planned to develop careers of their own before they married. She dreamed of how wonderful it would be to have an apartment that was all hers. She wished she were free to sign up for evening courses that interested her without worrying about being home in time to prepare supper for her husband.

Neither is sure exactly when it happened, but sometime during their freshman year of college, Eric and Greta began to fall out of love. Being married had become more of a burden than a joy for both of them. Each wanted to be free to grow, change, and date new people.

At first they decided to try a trial separation. Eric kept the apartment and Greta moved into the women's dormitory. Both went to the singles mingles offered by the school. Sometimes they met other people, other times they left together. The first few months were very awkward. It was as if they were marginal people who didn't feel comfortable married or single. As the months passed, however, they began to adjust.

When Mr. K., the anthropology professor, learned about their separation, he began taking Greta out. At first Greta was thrilled, but after a while she found that Mr. K. was more interested in talking about himself than in being with her.

She was also dismayed to learn that Mr. K. was dating a number of other young students besides herself. Greta felt disappointed and hurt. When she confronted Mr. K. with this information, he did not deny the fact, but politely reminded her that they had not made an agreement to see one another exclusively and that he was free to do as he pleased. Three weeks later, Greta terminated their relationship. She soon began dating another anthropology major, but did not become overly involved with the boy.

As for Eric, he too began acting on some of the secret desires he had during his marriage to Greta. He and Judy began seeing a great deal of each other. They even spent several spring weekends at the shore together. However, within two months, Judy left him for a graduate student.

It is interesting to note that both Greta and Eric suffered romantic disappointments after their separation. Nevertheless, they decided not to reunite but to go through with a divorce instead. As Greta put it, "Just because our later involvements didn't work out doesn't mean the marriage was right for us. Eric and I should have never married. We were just too young, but we didn't realize it. Right now I don't know if I'll ever remarry. I don't even know if I ever want children. The only thing that I'm certain of is that I want to be an anthropologist, and that requires a good deal of study that can interfere with marriage or any time-consuming relationship. I'm still not sure who I am as a person, so how can I try to be part of a couple yet?"

Eric and Greta did not have a bitter divorce. Greta waived her right to alimony, and the two split what little money they had in the bank between them. They parted as friends, but they saw very little of one another because, as it turned out, they really had nothing in common. Two years later both agreed that it was hard to believe that they were once married. Still, Eric claims that he's sorry it didn't work out and that he feels he'll always have a sense of failure about his first marriage.

Not every teenage marriage fails. Carol is a twenty-four-year-old housewife with four children who married at seventeen and managed to stay married. As Carol described her experience,

Well, we did it, but it certainly wasn't easy. I was seventeen and my husband George was eighteen when we tied the knot. We married the summer we both graduated high school and that meant college was out of the question for me. I went to work in an office as a clerk, but with only a high school diploma, I didn't earn very much. George worked too during the day, and at night he took college courses. I felt very lonely on the nights he went to class or stayed late at the library to study, but there was no money for tuition for me, and besides George promised to send me later. Yet, I think I should add that seven years have gone by, and I still haven't gotten my chance to go. In any case, those nights when George was away were the worst times for me. I kept feeling as though I was missing out on something.

We hadn't planned on having children until much later, but first came our daughter Kim, and a year later our son Brian was born. I don't know how I lived through it. While my friends were out giggling about their blind dates, I was home changing diapers. My mother worked all day, so she really wasn't very much help, and we couldn't afford babysitters. I wasn't able to work, so we lost my income, and George had to drop out of school and take a second job.

Money always seemed to be extremely scarce. With the two children we really needed a bigger apartment, but we were unable to move. That meant the four of us were forced to live in a one-bedroom apartment. With two cribs in the living room and an assortment of toys scattered across the floor, our home was hardly suitable for entertaining guests. George and I found that we felt ashamed to invite the few couples we did have as friends over. We became increasingly isolated and lonely. Being at home all day alone with the children was especially difficult for me.

Those years were the most trying ones of my life. Things gradually improved with time. George advanced on his job and consequently began to earn more money. He was able to return to night school to finish his degree. We had two more children, Elizabeth and Patrick, and I still can't figure out how it all happened so quickly.

With four children our living quarters had become unbearable. We had put aside a tiny nest egg for my college education. However, there were so many other pressing needs that I felt selfish about spending the money on myself. Instead we decided to use it toward the rent on a larger apartment, as well as for some new baby furniture.

I can't honestly say that I don't regret some of the decisions I made when I was seventeen. I love George and my children, but I've certainly had a hard time of it. Perhaps the most difficult thing for me was getting used to always having to do without. Few teenagers who marry have very much money. It's hard to all of a sudden be so different from all your friends. It's as if overnight your interests are miles apart. Being a mother in real life is very different from playing with dolls or even babysitting. It's a twenty-four-hour-a-day, seven-day-a-week job. For the first four years of my marriage, I thought I'd never get a full night's sleep. A baby must be fed every four hours around the clock. As soon as each of my children became old enough to sleep through the night, his younger brother or sister would wake him up crying for his food, and then the older child would start crying too. At times I've had all four children crying in unison. It's a regular chorus. The problem is that I only have two hands, and it's impossible to take care of everyone at once. Sometimes I feel like a marionette with strings pulling on me from all ends.

When you marry young you have to give up many of the things that are important to people your own age. I didn't realize that at the time of my wedding. Somehow, I felt certain that the love and security that comes from having a family of your own would make up for everything I missed. Yet when I hear about bicycling tours for young people going through Europe, I can't help wishing I could go too. Of course, that's impossible for me now. I still love George and my children, and I am certain that I want to spend the rest of my life with them. I just wish I had had time to accomplish a bit more on my own before I made this commitment.

CHAPTER 

Can Friendship Between a Boy and a Girl Survive?

Is it possible to maintain an ongoing friendship with a boy or a girl whom you aren't romantically interested in? It is true that most people tend to select members of their own sex for close friendships. Perhaps this is because they seem to have much more in common with such individuals; besides, such relationships are generally considered more acceptable. A boy/girl relationship that is platonic is often looked at skeptically. People may wonder if there isn't something going on after all. If they are aware that the relationship is not romantic in any way, they may wonder why those two people are always together. There's no doubt about it—boy/girl friendships are difficult to maintain. Some people, though, feel they are worth having.

Laurie, a high school junior, has a wonderful friendship with Brett, a senior she met through the school journalism club. They have no romantic interest in each other nor have they ever entertained any such notion. They simply like each other and enjoy one another's company. As Laurie described their relationship,

> Being friends with Brett was difficult at first. Not because of anything he or I did, it was simply that others tended not to accept our feelings for one another as legitimate friendship. Brett had it especially difficult. His other friends constantly teased him about being friends with a girl. They all said it was weird and suggested that Brett must be very desperate if he befriended a female. I think they were just jealous of all the good times and closeness we shared. In any case, Brett was strong enough to stand up to them, and recently the ridicule has somewhat subsided. Brett has by far the best sense of humor of anyone I know—male or female. He's so bright, witty, and funny that I've found that I've spent many of my happiest hours with him. His friendship means a great deal to me, and I wouldn't stop caring about Brett and being his friend for anything in the world.

Pam, a high school sophomore, has developed a wonderful friendship with Michael, her older brother's closest friend. Pam got to know Michael from the many hours he spent at her home visiting her brother. After a few months Pam and Michael found that they liked being together. Michael soon realized that often when he had arranged to see Pam's brother, he either arrived at the house earlier or managed to leave later in order to spend some time with Pam. To Michael, Pam was the younger sister he had never had. In Michael, Pam found an older brother who showed more kindness and interest in her than her own biological brother.

Both Pam and Michael loved to go horseback riding, and they spent Saturday afternoons together riding. Once Pam began dating, Michael's friendship helped her a lot. It was great to get a bird's-eye view into the male psyche. Michael was always willing to tell Pam his opinions about the various tactics employed by the girls he knew. These candid insights were very helpful to Pam in formulating her own behavior toward boys. Michael was also very open and informative in offering his opinion on specific situations Pam brought to his attention. Pam soon found that his friendship helped to give her the self-confidence she needed to feel more at ease with boys her own age. Michael and Pam felt very lucky to have one another, and their friendship lasted for several years.

It isn't always easy to initiate a genuine friendship with a member of the opposite sex. Since the beginning of the school term, Karen, a high school freshman, had developed a crush on Doug, a senior at her school. After several months of diligent effort, Karen was forced to realize that Doug was probably never going to ask her out for a date. Doug generally dated only junior and senior girls, and usually they were both very beautiful and popular. However, Karen still thought Doug was a great guy, and she sincerely hoped they could be friends.

Although most people might think that anyone would be glad to have a new friend, this was not the case with Doug. At first, he felt very flattered that Karen idolized him and spent most of her time after school trying to be with him. After a few weeks, Doug began to get abusive. He managed to forget the arrangements he had made to meet Karen at various places—once she waited for over two hours for Doug at a record shop, but he never arrived. He'd be with Karen when there was nothing better to do, but as soon as a more desirable alternative appeared, he was quick to discard her.

It soon became clear to Karen that Doug was unable to treat her as an equal and offer her real friendship. Although Karen did her best to overcome any obstacle that stood in the way of their friendship, Doug simply refused to take her seriously. Eventually, Karen dropped Doug. She had finally decided that she was definitely not interested in humiliation and second-class treatment.

Often girl/boy platonic friendships are ruined if one person develops romantic sentiments that are not shared by the other. Elaine, a high school freshman, had developed a wonderful friendship with Kenny, a sophomore she had met through a filmmaking workshop at her local library. The two became friends after months of working together on film projects. One of their shorts even won first prize in a local competition.

Kenny and Elaine greatly admired each other. They often had similar ideas regarding what they wanted to film, and when they came up with the same shooting techniques without consulting one another, they joked about sharing one mind between them. At times, Kenny would teasingly say that they were turning into twins. Kenny and Elaine began to spend a lot of time together. They spent quite a few Saturdays biking and hiking. Elaine especially enjoyed the special picnics she planned. She always made it a point to remember to pack Kenny's favorite foods.

As time passed their friendship continued to grow. There wasn't anything they couldn't discuss. That is, until Dirk came into Elaine's life.

Dirk was a senior from a neighboring school whom Elaine had met at a church dance. She was quite taken with him. As the two began dating, Elaine's feelings for Dirk deepened. She spent many hours on the telephone telling her friends how happy she was to have found Dirk. Kenny was no exception. She described Dirk in glorious detail to her filmmaking friend and expected him to applaud her for her good taste in men.

After a short time, Kenny began to feel irritated whenever Elaine spoke about Dirk, but he wasn't quite sure why. He found that he was constantly comparing himself to Dirk, and he daydreamed about situations in which he outsmarted Dirk or was superior to him in athletic feats. Before long Kenny realized what was happening to him. It wasn't that he disliked Dirk, but rather that he liked Elaine. He was certain that he cared for Elaine not only as a friend, but as a girl.

At first Kenny felt embarrassed by his real feelings. Elaine and he had never thought about having a romance. In fact, they had always been much more like brother and sister. Elaine too had been disturbed by Kenny's recent behavior. She greatly valued Kenny's friendship and couldn't understand why he always seemed to be insulting Dirk with little provocation. She noticed a distinct change in Kenny's attitude but had no idea of what was happening.

After a few weeks of trying to deny what was happening to him, Kenny decided to tell Elaine how he really felt about her. She was quite taken aback by the news—Elaine felt very confused by the entire situation. She knew she loved Kenny, but only as a friend. She was not physically attracted to him and felt that she never could be. She felt as though she were falling in love with Dirk, but she still cherished Kenny's friendship and trust. She wanted both of them, but in very different ways.

Elaine was quite honest with Kenny regarding her feelings about him. She had a great deal of respect for Kenny and felt that he deserved a direct answer. Kenny was hurt, but thanked Elaine for her honesty. The two mutually decided that they meant too much to each other to stop seeing one another. They agreed to continue their friendship.

However, things did not go as smoothly as they had planned. Kenny tried to squelch his romantic interest in Elaine, but that was easier said than done. Instead of going away, his jealousy of Dirk intensified. Every time he saw Elaine and Dirk together, Kenny was filled with anger. To worsen matters, his initial attraction to Elaine deepened. To him, she seemed to grow more beautiful every day. He wanted very much to kiss her, but he had to constantly hold himself back.

Kenny and Elaine's relationship became strained. Tensions mounted as they tried to continue the friendship that had once come to them so naturally. Small incidents began to be magnified out of proportion. Every time Kenny as much as touched Elaine, she accused him of making advances. Each time Elaine spent an afternoon with Dirk, Kenny accused her of ignoring him and their film projects. Elaine and Kenny began to argue more and more often. Much of the joy they had experienced in their former relationship vanished.

Acknowledging that they were no longer able to work together, Kenny and Elaine now created independent film projects. However, it soon became so painful for Kenny to see Elaine that he dropped out of the film workshop completely. Elaine called him to encourage him not to give up film making and to return to the workshop, but Kenny insisted that it was just too much for him.

Elaine and Kenny's friendship eventually dissolved completely. It was no longer possible for them to get along well together, and although each went out of his way to avoid the other, for many months both greatly missed the bond of friendship they had once shared.

Jealousy can break up friendships when another type of triangle arises as well. Stan, a premed student at a local college, had dated Irene, a high school senior, for about a year and a half before they broke up. Irene and Stan had enjoyed more than romance during the time they spent together; they had developed a beautiful friendship. When the love light between them dimmed, Stan and Irene decided they still wanted to remain in one another's life in some way.

Stan always asked Irene, who had excellent taste, to go with him when he went shopping for clothes. They often went to the movies together or on bicycling tours. At several points during their new relationship, Irene began to have second thoughts. She told Stan that she missed having him as a boyfriend and asked if things could not be as they once were between them. In a very kind way, Stan explained to her that whatever he once felt for her romantically was gone. Over the past few months, Irene had put on a good deal of weight, and Stan was no longer physically attracted to her. However, he said that he hoped they could always be friends. Irene agreed to this.

Time passed and things went along well enough until Stan began dating Ellen, a classmate of Irene's at school. Ellen was a trim, pert, pretty girl with a wonderful personality. Although Irene and Stan were now just friends, Irene couldn't help feeling a twinge of jealousy. She felt like a blimp next to Ellen. It is ironic that it was Ellen, not Irene, who underwent the severest pangs of jealousy over what she believed to be a triangle. Although Stan had repeatedly assured Ellen that nothing was going on between him and Irene, Ellen seemed to doubt Stan's sincerity. She noticed that Stan and Irene still spent a good deal of time together. Also, Stan usually seemed very happy in Irene's company. Irene had a wonderful sense of humor and always managed to keep Stan laughing. Even Ellen enjoyed Irene's jokes, but her jealousy tended to diminish the pleasure of the experience.

As Irene and Ellen were classmates, they tended to leave school at about the same time every day. When Stan came to pick up Ellen, he'd also offer Irene a ride home if he saw her passing by. Stan felt this gesture was simply a matter of good manners, but his politeness infuriated Ellen. She felt that Irene was constantly intruding upon their relationship. Frequently they'd all end up going for sodas or shopping together.

Ellen wanted a romance, but she felt as though she were destined to deal with a happy threesome instead. When the three were together, Stan never made romantic overtures to Ellen. She often complained that he wouldn't even hold hands with her. Ellen clearly understood that an overt demonstration of affection between them might make Irene feel uncomfortable, but she still very much wanted to prove both to herself and Irene that she was now Stan's girl.

Ellen's friends were not very sympathetic to her plight. They thought it was disgraceful that Stan still saw so much of Irene while he was going with Ellen, and they were not bashful about revealing such sentiments to Ellen. A number of people even insinuated to Ellen that Stan and Irene were still secretly involved with one another.

Ellen viewed Stan's friendship with Irene as a source of humiliation to her. She was also forced to contend with her own doubts and feelings of jealousy. After a few months, she confronted Stan directly about the situation. Ellen chose to deliver a very painful ultimatum to Stan—either he give up his friendship with Irene or he and Ellen stop seeing each other.

Stan felt torn by Ellen's reaction. He didn't want to lose Ellen, but he was angry at her for trying to exert control over his life. He believed that Ellen was being juvenile and petty, and he wished that she were understanding enough to allow him to enjoy both her love and Irene's friendship. When he expressed these feelings to Ellen, she firmly told him that the only friendships she was willing to tolerate were those he shared with other boys. Stan felt suffocated by Ellen's attitude, but their relationship meant more to him than Irene's friendship.

When Stan told Irene that he would not be able to see her anymore, she cried bitterly. She told Stan that she did not know what she had done to merit such treatment. When Stan assured her that she had done nothing, she cried even harder. Irene kept repeating that their relationship had been totally innocent, and that there was no valid reason for her to be cast off like a piece of old clothing. Stan knew she was right and felt very guilty about his own behavior.

With a great deal of anguish, Stan finally did manage to break off his relationship with Irene. He simply told himself that it was impossible to have a friendship with one girl and a romance with another at the same time. It is ironic that Stan and Ellen broke up only a few months later. Neither Stan nor Ellen knew exactly why it happened. It just seemed to both of them that they spent too much time arguing and not enough time enjoying one another's company. It is difficult to figure out why their relationship disintegrated so quickly. However, Stan did tell one of his closest friends that he could never quite bring himself to forgive Ellen for not allowing him to share a meaningful friendship with a very special person who just happened to be a girl.

Individuals who attempt to pursue friendships with members of the opposite sex are bound to experience some awkwardness in various situations. Yet a good friend who enriches your experiences and shares pleasures with you is difficult to find. If you are fortunate enough to have any such wonderful individuals in your life, don't concern yourself over whether they are male or female—just enjoy their friendship and work to preserve it.

CHAPTER 7

Special Kindnesses That Show You Care

Marsha is a twenty-one-year-old college senior. She is engaged to marry a wonderful young dentist whom she loves very dearly. Marsha's fiancé has bought her a great number of gifts over the past few years. Her most treasured possession is a small golden tooth that hangs from her charm bracelet. Harvey had crafted the tooth for her from a mold he had worked with in dentistry school. He made it for Marsha during a week in which he was too busy with examinations and patients to see her. Harvey wanted Marsha to know that even while he was overworked she was still in his thoughts. He sent it to Marsha in a small black velvet jewelry box with a note that read, "For the girl with the golden smile." Marsha appreciated the gift because it was funny, personal, and uniquely Harvey.

How can you show someone you care about how much he or she means to you? The ways are as limitless as your imagination. It's easy enough to send a birthday card or a Christmas present, but at times gifts selected for designated occasions lack spontaneity and individuality. If, for some reason, you are forced to shop for ten Christmas gifts when there are only five days left before the holiday, it's likely that you won't have sufficient time to give some careful thought to each present.

A delightful present need not be a tangible object, and it doesn't have to be given on a specific day. Time spent together can also be a beautiful gesture. Kathy, a high school sophomore from Pennsylvania, had been dating Bill, a senior, for about six months. They had arranged to go on a hayride sponsored by the youth organization of their church on Saturday night, when Bill got sick during the week. A visit to the doctor confirmed that Bill had the mumps. Bill would not be able to go on the hayride, and he would also have to stay out of school for a while. He was a very outgoing person who hated the idea of being bedridden. He knew he'd miss school, his friends, and especially Kathy.

Kathy, who had already had the mumps, sympathized with Bill's discomfort. She wanted to do something to make him feel better, so she made arrangements with Bill to be at his house promptly at 7:30 P.M. the Saturday evening of the hayride. On Saturday afternoon she cooked all of Bill's favorite foods—a meatloaf made with nuts and raisins, candied sweet potatoes, and pecan pie. She carefully wrapped the meal in a red and white checkered tablecloth and put it in a picnic basket. When she arrived at his house, Kathy and Bill had a candlelight picnic on the floor of Bill's finished basement. Bill was delighted with Kathy's creativity and concern, even though he couldn't eat very well.

There are many simple ways to show that someone special is in your thoughts. If you read a newspaper or magazine article that might be of interest, clip it out and send it to that person through the mail. A funny cartoon arriving in an envelope guarantees a smile as well. When you do give a gift on a special occasion, such as Christmas or a birthday, make it a very personal item. If you knit, knit him a scarf in his favorite color. If you're skilled in carpentry, make a miniature bookshelf for her paperback books.

It's always fun to have a cake delivered to your front door before school on your birthday. Surprise birthday parties take a great deal of work, energy, and planning, but they are usually well remembered and appreciated.

If the person you love is swamped with a great deal of work for a special paper or project, support his or her trips to the library with a library visit of your own. Go through some older issues of periodicals to see if any articles might prove helpful. Make a short list of the most relevant books the library owns pertaining to the topic and give it to your friend. Make friends with the librarian, she'll prove to be a very helpful person to you both. If your friend is completely exhausted or overburdened with other work by the time the paper is finished, offer to type it up.

If a special person in your life would like to be with you, but can't because he or she must study for an examination, stop by the house to deliver a pint of his or her favorite flavor of ice cream. Stay only long enough to make the delivery—remember, you are trying to help the person, not distract him from his studies.

If your friend is away at college, call him at a time you suspect he'll need it most. Weekends are often a good time to call, since people away from home tend to feel most lonely then. Make sure to call him on his birthday or after an important examination that you know he spent a good deal of time studying for. Just the sound of your voice will make him feel wonderful. Long distance telephone calls can become quite expensive. Be aware of what you are spending, and to help keep costs down, make the calls from a pay phone near your home. Gather up a fair amount of change, and when your money runs out, say good-bye, throw a kiss, and hang up. With this method you'll be able to make many more calls.

Perhaps the most meaningful way to show someone you care is to lend support at a difficult time or when the person is going through an especially trying experience. If her parents are getting a divorce, try to realize what she's going through. Make certain you have time to be a sympathetic listener and hear how she feels. Take him out to lunch after he's been through a grueling interview for a job he wants. The day she learns that she didn't make the cheerleading squad buy her a slice of pizza and a Coke and tell her she's terrific. If he spent his entire month's allowance for a new jacket he wanted, offer to pay your own way on a date.

If she's a very heavy smoker, carry a small supply of candy with you when you know you are going to be together. Every time she's about to light a cigarette offer her a piece of candy or a stick of gum instead. If he loves chocolate chip cookies or caramel apples, make up a batch and present them to him to celebrate any occasion at all. Take your favorite picture of the two of you and have it silk screened on a T-shirt for her birthday. If she's busy studying for an exam, finishing a paper, or even preparing to go to a big dance with you, offer to help her with some of the little things that may clutter her life. Give her a few free moments by offering to walk her dog, clean out the fish tank, or babysit with her younger brother.

If she has to work late and then must take a long walk or bus ride home, surprise her by picking her up after work. Even if you don't have a car to drive her home in, the trip will go much faster if the two of you are together. If you go away on a trip with your family, send him a different picture postcard for every day you are away. Return his books to the library the day before they are due to save him from paying the fines.

Make a collage for him to hang in his room. For materials, use pictures of the two of you together. If she's trying to diet, take her to the nearest health food store instead of the pizza parlor. Wrap his gift in wrapping paper you designed yourself. If he's experiencing difficulty adhering to his jogging schedule, get up early before school and jog with him.

Bicycle with him to his favorite picnic spot and bring a picnic basket containing all the foods he likes best.

Gary, a high school junior, and Sonia, a sophomore, had been going together for over a year and had a good relationship. Sonia meant a great deal to Gary, who was very appreciative of her love and feelings for him. Gary always tried to cushion Sonia's disappointments with little surprises. When Sonia didn't get the lead role she had tried out for in the school play, Gary presented her with a small rock he had painted and named Sonnie. When Sonia received a C on her English paper after she had been hoping for an A, Gary bought her a stick of shimmering gold eye shadow to wear to the disco on Saturday night. When she broke her rib after falling down while roller-skating, Gary brought her a lovely flowered barrette for her hair. Gary did not have a great deal of money to spend on Sonia's gifts, but it didn't matter. At different times, Gary presented Sonia with small tokens of his feelings for her, and Sonia adored him for his kindness and thoughtful deeds.

No relationship is valid without a bond of friendship between the two people. Being a friend does not mean you must shower the other person with expensive luxuries. It means caring about another person and showing that person how much he or she means to you in special ways. It's very important never to forget that the best way to make a friend is to be a friend.

CHAPTER 8

Going Steady

Going steady generally means exclusive dating—the two people agree to date no one else. As with any other dating situation, going steady offers both pluses and minuses.

Some young people view going steady as a symbol of guaranteed popularity. When you are going steady with someone, you are assured of a date for all important occasions. You know you are going to the prom, parties, and special school events with someone who cares about you in a very special way. As Margie, a high school junior, described it, "Lenny and I have been going steady for almost five months now. I feel very good about having Lenny as my steady boyfriend. He's tall, a senior, and owns his own car. It's such a pleasure not to have to run after guys anymore. Lenny is always there, and I love it. It's great not to have to sit by the telephone, wondering if anyone is going to call you up to ask you out.

Lenny took a lot of stress and worry out of my life. I feel as though I have a lot more strength and energy now. Instead of spending all my spare time flirting with guys, now I have more hours in which to study and become more active in sports."

The security going steady offers can be a trap as well as a blessing. It's very important not to rush into a steady relationship because you are afraid no one else will ask you out. Jenny, a high school sophomore, moved to Los Angeles with her family from a small town in southern California. A very shy girl, Jenny had always had difficulty meeting new people and making friends. Surrounded by so many other girls, Jenny felt certain that no one would ever ask her out again. She was beginning to despair about it when she met Bruce, a junior at the same school.

Bruce took an instant liking to Jenny. He said she had a helpless, vulnerable quality about her that he found very appealing. He often told others that he felt Jenny needed him to take care of her. Bruce soon began walking Jenny home and asking her out every night of the week. Jenny felt very flattered by all this attention and allowed Bruce to move into her life. She wasn't quite sure whether or not she was ready for a serious relationship, but she felt very relieved that someone had noticed her and seemed to care for her a great deal. When Bruce asked her to go steady with him three weeks later, she accepted his ring.

At first Jenny seemed to bask in Bruce's affection. She no longer had to worry about popularity; now she was assured of an escort to all social functions. Sometimes she felt saddened by the fact that her romantic interest in Bruce was not terribly overpowering, but he made her feel secure, and for a shy girl in a new school this was tremendously important.

However, as time passed, Jenny's situation changed. She started to feel more confident about herself and began making new friends. Now she was invited to parties, and sometimes she wished she didn't always have to bring Bruce. She wanted to dance with the other boys and get to know them better. The predicament began to worsen when a number of the boys at her school began to take an active interest in Jenny. Some would express their disappointment that Jenny was already going with someone, while others would actively encourage her to break up with Bruce.

About a month after this, Jenny and Bruce did break up. Jenny told Bruce truthfully, that she now felt too fenced in and wanted to see other boys. Bruce felt angry and hurt by the episode. He accused Jenny of using him and said that if she felt that way she had had no right to go steady with him in the first place. Jenny felt guilty about her actions because she knew Bruce was right. Still, she felt she had no alternative other than to end the relationship. She hoped that Bruce would still date her casually, but he would have nothing to do with her.

Before you make the commitment to go steady with anyone, make certain that is exactly what you want to do. Marie, a high school sophomore from Detroit, was happy dating her boyfriend Frank and occasionally enjoying dates with other boys. However, Frank was of an extremely jealous nature and deeply resented Marie's encounters with other boys

He wanted to know that Marie belonged to him and wanted Marie to feel the same way.

Marie felt that she was too young and inexperienced to become deeply involved with anyone. She did not care for Frank's possessiveness, but she liked other traits about him and did not want to give him up. Therefore, when Frank firmly insisted that he and Marie go steady, Marie agreed to it. After accepting Frank's offer, Marie found herself being unhappy for many months. Unfortunately, she wasn't able to get up the courage to break up with him.

Going steady can never offer a couple a guarantee of happiness, but there is a good way of exploring the whole process of becoming close to another person. It's sort of a close-up view of what a permanent, monogamous relationship would be like. The participants are offered the opportunity to deal with both the pain and pleasure that intimacy brings. Donna and Harry, two seniors from New York City, went steady for most of their last year of high school. Although they broke up in April of their senior year, both are glad they tried it.

As Donna explained,

> Harry and I planned to get married immediately after graduation. It would have been a terrible mistake. Now we're both glad we were able to avoid it. Going steady made us see that we weren't right for each other. It also helped me realize that I wasn't ready to get married.
>
> The responsibility of going steady meant a lot more than just having a steady boyfriend. I felt I had to meet all of Harry's needs, and frankly sometimes listening to

his problems all day bored me. We found that it was often difficult to work out differences between us. Harry saw things one way, I saw them another way, and at times we're both very stubborn. I think I liked the idea of going steady more than I liked the actual process. Somehow wearing someone's ring made me feel very special. But the whole thing just wasn't worth the effort.

When two people decide to go steady, there are always questions that must be worked out. How much time will they devote to one another? How will expenses be shared? How far will they go sexually? How will they work out disputes equitably? It is important not to go steady until you feel absolutely ready to undertake the experience. A boy who feels he has to date every attractive young woman he meets might feel very trapped going steady, even if he deeply cares for the girl he gives his ring to. It is also wise to try to date a lot of people before deciding to go steady with anyone. This experience will help you determine what you're looking for in a dating partner.

If you do decide to go steady, try to deal with your new relationship maturely. Don't expect to win every argument, but stand up for what you believe in. Remember that you are an equal partner in the relationship and that you have an obligation to yourself to make certain that your opinion is heard.

Going steady is a practice relationship of sorts. Some people regard it as a preview of the more serious relationships that come later in life. Fortunately for its young participants, going steady does not have the permanence of marriage. It's an experiment for two people who wish to spend a good deal of time together and date one another exclusively. It is important not to feel hemmed in by your new status once you have agreed to do this. Going steady is a good choice for you only as long as it fulfills your needs. Remember that although it is important to experience a deep, intense, emotional relationship with someone special before you choose a marriage partner, it is equally important to date a good number of people, so you'll be certain of what you really want in a spouse.

After her freshman year of college, Joan married the boy she had gone steady with all through high school. A year later Joan was divorced. Joan explained it this way,

> It wasn't that I didn't love Mark. Believe me, I really did. It was just that I had only dated two other boys in my entire life. Here I was a married woman on campus, listening to my girl friends talk about the new guys they were meeting and how exciting they were. I started to feel as though I had missed something very special. It was as though an entire part of my life had been deleted. I tried not to, but now I seemed constantly to find fault with Mark—nothing he did pleased me. We argued often. I just couldn't help wondering if I could be better suited to someone else. I'm sorry it had to happen, but we just couldn't live together any longer. The divorce seemed inevitable. I have a lot of catching up to do. There are countless dates I want to go on before I once again make a permanent decision.

It is highly likely that you'll have a number of dates with different people throughout the period of your young adulthood. You may even have the opportunity to go steady a number of times. Whatever you choose for yourself, it is important to make certain that your decisions are guided not by status requirements, but by your own needs and feelings.

CHAPTER 

Sexual Involvement

For many years, sex was considered a forbidden subject. Any discussions of it were whispered ones, and written material on the subject was generally reserved for married people. Perhaps all the secrecy was intended to keep the young innocent, but it also kept them ignorant. Contrary to the old saying, "ignorance is bliss," ignorance is dangerous.

It is essential that every young woman know how her reproductive organs operate and how conception takes place. When a woman is born, her body contains all the eggs or ova it will ever release. The eggs remain undeveloped in her ovaries, which are two small organs outside her uterus. The uterus is a small hollow organ that resembles an inverted pear. The Fallopian tubes, two long pipelike passageways, lie adjacent to the ovaries. Each month a single egg passes through one or the other of these tubes to the uterus. If the egg is fertilized by the male sperm during sexual intercourse, it remains in the uterus where it grows to become an embryo and finally a fetus.

The tip of the uterus is at the cervix, which contains a small opening and extends slightly into the vagina. The woman's vagina acts as a passageway joining her internal reproductive organs with her outside. The area between the walls of the vagina will expand to hold the penis during intercourse or the baby as it passes through the uterus during birth.

At puberty, a woman's reproductive organs mature. A cycle of monthly activity begins which will last for approximately the next thirty-five years. The cycle is set in motion when the pituitary gland produces a certain hormone which begins a series of events in the ovaries.

First, several follicles in the ovaries, each holding an egg, begin to grow larger, while the remaining follicles do not change. Estrogen, another hormone, is released by the growing follicles. Estrogen makes the lining of the uterus thicken to form a soft nourishing surface for the egg to implant itself on should it become fertilized. The follicles continue their growth for about a week, until one becomes larger than the others. This follicle increases its growth, while the others return to their former size. Ovulation occurs on the fourteenth day of the cycle, when the enlarged follicle breaks apart to release the egg.

The egg quickly travels down one of the Fallopian tubes. If fertilization is to take place, it will occur between twenty-four and thirty-six hours after the egg has been released. If fertilization doesn't occur, the hormonal level drops as the thick uterus lining is no longer necessary. This process sends a message back to the pituitary gland to start the next cycle. Menstrual blood will wash away the unfertilized egg and the unused lining. In the ovaries new follicles will once again begin to grow.

One well-known established agency that offers information on conception and its control as well as on venereal disease is the Planned Parenthood Federation of America. Planned Parenthood has approximately 260 branches in over 40 states. Planned Parenthood centers are situated in many major cities as well as in some smaller locales. The organization's largest branch is in New York City. Planned Parenthood provides a number of services to teenage women. In educational sessions at Planned Parenthood, a young woman can learn about the various methods by which reproduction can be controlled. It is very important for the user to completely understand efficiency, side effects, and any risks involved with a given method of birth control.

The pill is the most effective method of birth control. Using synthetic hormones, similar to those produced by a woman's body, the pill prevents ovulation. It also affects the uterine lining, making it difficult for the fertilized egg to implant itself in the uterus. A woman takes one pill a day for a specific number of days, depending upon the type of pill. For the pill to be effective, it must be taken every day. A woman will not be protected against pregnancy if she takes only one pill immediately after intercourse. What is needed is the total effect of all the pills in the packet to prevent ovulation during the entire month.

Perhaps the pill's greatest advantage is its high rate of effectiveness. Also, a woman does not have to interrupt lovemaking to use it, and she may feel more relaxed about sex because her chances of becoming pregnant are so minimal.

There are disadvantages to the pill. Some women experience unpleasant side effects such as nausea and fatigue, while others forget to take it every day. A minority of women have more serious complications such as migraine headaches, weight gain, or blood clots. Some of the side effects may be eliminated by switching to a different brand of pill. Some women must stop taking the pill immediately.

The pill should never be used by any woman who has ever experienced inflammation of the veins, blood clots, serious liver disease, or cancer of the uterus or breast. The pill may or may not be acceptable for a woman who has heart disease, kidney disease, high blood pressure, diabetes, epilepsy, fibroids of the uterus, migraine headaches, or serious visual problems.

The pill should not be confused with the morning after pill, which in reality is one large dose of estrogen given to a woman between twenty-four and thirty-six hours after unprotected intercourse to prevent pregnancy from settling in. The morning after pill is still not widely accepted, though.

Another popular birth control device is the IUD or Intra-Uterine Device. An IUD is a device placed in a woman's uterus by a physician. It is usually made of plastic and is available in several shapes. It is still unknown why the IUD is so effective or exactly how it works. Yet it prevents pregnancy for 97 percent of the women whose bodies are able to retain it. Until it is removed by a physician, the IUD remains in the woman's body. Many IUDs come equipped with slender nylon threads or beads that allow the woman to check that her IUD is still properly inserted and has not been expelled.

The IUD does not interfere with a woman's body chemistry. There are generally no side effects except for rare cases of pelvic infection. As with the pill, it does not interfere with intercourse.

However, close to 40 percent of the women who have tried IUDs find that they are unable to tolerate them. In most cases, either the woman's body expels it or it must be removed because it causes pain or discomfort to the woman. A majority of women will experience cramps after the initial insertion of an IUD, but for some women cramps and heavy bleeding during periods will continue for several months. Occasionally, a woman who cannot tolerate one type of IUD will feel perfectly comfortable with another.

Another effective method of birth control for women who feel comfortable with it is the diaphragm used with spermicidal cream or jelly. The woman inserts the diaphragm, which is a thin rubber cup, into her body by herself to block the opening between the uterus and the vagina. The woman first spreads some spermicidal cream or jelly on both sides of the diaphragm before inserting it. In this manner she is doubly protected against pregnancy—the sperm are blocked from entering the uterus by the cup as well as chemically killed by the cream or jelly. Although the woman inserts the diaphragm herself each time before intercourse, she must initially be fitted for it by a physician. Once the diaphragm is properly inserted, it will not slip out of place and cannot be felt by either the man or the woman during intercourse. After intercourse, the woman must not remove the diaphragm for at least six hours.

The diaphragm is a method of birth control that works well, is completely painless, and has no side effects. Some women find it bothersome to insert it each time before intercourse, as it interrupts love-making. A diaphragm is still effective enough if inserted up to three hours before intercourse.

Condoms or prophylactics are a contraceptive method used by the male. Condoms are made of sheaths of very thin rubber or animal membranes which fit snuggly over the penis to prevent sperm from flowing into the woman's vagina. It is important to put the condom on before the penis enters the vagina because often drops of semen which contain sperm are secreted before the male reaches orgasm. Condoms tend to be a popular birth control method, as they are available in drugstores without a prescription, are inexpensive, and have no harmful side effects for either the man or the woman. However, there are some people who feel that such protective shields cut down on their sexual enjoyment.

There are additional methods of birth control available, but their rate of effectiveness is not very high. Among these are vaginal foams, creams, or jellies used alone. These are sperm killers, which may be purchased at a drugstore without a prescription, and must be inserted into the woman's vagina just prior to intercourse. There are generally no negative side effects, although occasionally the cream or jelly may irritate the man's penis or the woman's vagina. However, the risk of becoming pregnant is significant.

When a couple employs withdrawal as a method of birth control, the man withdraws his penis from the woman's vagina before he has an orgasm. Perhaps the main advantage of this method is that it is free and requires no prior preparation. It is not very safe because of the drops of semen, containing sperm, excreted by some males prior to orgasm.

If a woman decides to use the rhythm method of birth control, she must determine when ovulation occurs and abstain from intercourse on the days she risks becoming pregnant. In order to use the rhythm method with any degree of effectiveness, a woman must have a fairly regular menstrual cycle. However, even with the aid of a doctor, calendar, and accurate accounts of her body temperature and monthly menstrual periods, it is still extremely difficult to determine on which days she can safely have intercourse.

Decisions as to how far to go sexually are very personal and often quite difficult to make. Sexual intercourse is perhaps the most meaningful way possible to express your love and depth of sentiment for another human being. It is not an act to be taken casually. Although its abuse is common, individuals who regard lovemaking as little more than a kiss miss much of its meaning and value.

It is extremely important never to be goaded into any gesture of affection by pressures from your friends or dates. If you don't feel like holding hands in the movies, simply take your hand away. Pay attention to your own feelings, and if you don't feel ready to show your good feelings about someone in a particular manner, don't do it. If the person you are with is so overly impatient that he can't understand how you feel, you are better off without him. It is crucial to feel comfortable about engaging in any act of love, no matter how insignificant it may be. If a boy pays for your dinner and then takes you to a movie, and you don't feel like giving him anymore than a good night kiss, do that, thanking him for a lovely evening. Don't expect any more from yourself. Obligation can only cheapen affection.

Every day we see newspaper headlines that read something like, "VD SKYROCKETING AMONG TEENAGERS," "PREGNANCY SIGNIFICANT FACTOR IN HIGH SCHOOL DROP OUT RATE," "ABORTIONS AMONG TEENAGE WOMEN REACH NEW HEIGHT."

While it may be correct that significant numbers of young people are having sex today, many are refusing to go along. If it's true that nearly one-half of today's young people have engaged in sexual intercourse, it is equally certain that more than half have not.

It is essential that you never lose track of what's right for you. Many teens appear eager to have sex, yet at the same time feel hesitant about it. Having sex before you're ready to love someone in that manner can be regrettable. If you don't want to have intercourse yet, just remember that there are millions of others like yourself who feel the same way.

Be honest about your sexual feelings. When discussing sex with your friends, say exactly what you really mean. At first it may appear easier to pretend. Remember that there may be other people who share your sentiments, but feel too afraid of condemnation to speak up.

Today many people are engaging in sex for all the wrong reasons. In fact, none of the following reasons for having sex has anything to do with loving or having a relationship with someone.

Using sex as a way of trying to feel less lonely or unhappy.

Using sex to try to become more popular among members of the opposite sex.

Using sex to prove that you are not a homosexual.

Using sex as a means to discovering the thrills that often accompany such exploits in books or in the cinema.

Using sex as a way to assert your independence from your parents and their values.

In reality, sexual intercourse will not resolve any of the above situations. If pursued in that manner it may even result in profound disappointment. Sexuality is extremely complex. If you sometimes feel confused, try talking to people you respect and trust —those at home, in school, at your church or synagogue, or in a medical setting. If you don't feel able to discuss sex with your parents, your church or synagogue may have some family life courses or group discussions. Some communities even have telephone hotlines staffed by counselors prepared to deal with sexual questions. Your school sex education program may also include discussions on intimacy and sexuality.

Remember that each individual must make up his or her own mind and live with those choices. Have confidence in your own decisions, and when you've gone as far as you want to go, say, "no."

Bibliography

Duvall, Evelyn M., and Johnson, Joy D. *Art of Dating.* Chicago: Association Press, 1967.

Landis, Paul H. *Your Dating Days: Looking Forward to Successful Marriage.* New York: McGraw, 1971.

Lipke, Jean C. *Dating.* Minneapolis: Lerner, 1971.

Peck, Ellen. *How to Get a Teenage Boy and What to Do With Him Once You Get Him.* New York: Avon, 1974.

Riemer, G.R. *Dating; Communication and Decision-Making.* New York: Holt, Rinehart & Winston, 1970.

Wood, Abigail. *The Seventeen Book of Answers to What Your Parents Won't Talk About & Your Best Friends Can't Tell You.* New York: McKay, 1972.

Index

ABOUT THE AUTHOR

Elaine Landau received her BA degree from New York University and her master's degree in Library and Information Science from Pratt Institute. She worked on the editorial staff of a children's book publishing company and as a youth services librarian before becoming Director of Tuckahoe Public Library in Tuckahoe, New York.

301.41/LAN 40-06767